THE 6 SALES HABITS

THE 6 SALES HABITS

Mastering the Ways of the
Sales Professional

JOE CONNELLY

The 6 Sales Habits: Mastering the Ways of the Sales Professional

DEDICATION

This book is dedicated to my mum and dad who both consistently encouraged me to "Do the best you can." Thank-you to both of you for having the patience and faith in me. I love you both!

CONTENTS

The Influencing Habit

The Balancing Habit

PREFACE

Welcome to the wonderful world of sales. Know that you are in a great place, with great people, great companies, and great prospects—in fact, the world truly is your oyster!

Sales is very much like life, where you have to create the right strategy, discover deep determination, and most importantly, develop an ongoing ability to learn and change. This book addresses the real-world challenges that all professional salespeople encounter at some point in their careers. The challenges remain basically the same, but overcoming them can yield the rewards of great salesmanship, including an accelerated career and rapid financial gain.

The topics, ideas, stories, and tools contained here are based on my own life in sales and marketing over the past 28 years. I have been fortunate to have worked and lived in six countries (Scotland, England, USA, Hong Kong, Canada, and Switzerland), as well as work for large multinational, mid-cap, and small-size companies, right down to starting a few companies of my own. I have been in sales, sales management, and executive sales management and currently coach senior sales executives to solve their biggest challenges and achieve even higher levels of performance—I guess you could say I have a long-lasting love affair with all things sales! What I have found remarkable, though, is that sales challenges appear to have the same basis, the same need to be solved, and a profound consistency across companies, industries, and countries.

My personal belief is that sales, like any job function, can be mastered by the proper application of courage, learning, change, and tenacity. Great salespeople can be outgoing and gregarious or shy and introverted—it's not the character but instead the characteristics that are important. The ones that day-in and day-out are used to tackle the many and exciting challenges that all sales roles exhibit today. Whether you are new to sales or a seasoned sales professional or entrepreneur, you will routinely experience great successes and bend to stinging disappointments, but not normally in equal measure. However, know that once you taste that initial sales success and internalize those feelings, it becomes like a positive drug that you want more of—and normally a lot more of. Welcome to the great allure and excitement of sales!

I also know at this stage that one thing is certain—if you want to be successful in sales, really want to be in the Top 1%, and are willing to go for it, then YOU CAN! Just decide that you really want to, and together let us explore the most important skills and habits necessary for accelerated sales success.

INTRODUCTION

"Knowledge is a process of piling up facts; wisdom lies in their simplification."
Rev. Dr. Martin Luther King Jr.

As I started to write this book, my overwhelming priority was to write and share in a way that was based on real-world practicality and simplicity. The information, teachings, and stories contained here are based on my many years of being in sales and marketing, having managed, mentored, and coached a wide range of people and personalities all over the world. It's also about the big challenges that are real for everyone who embarks on a sales career, but that tend not to be openly discussed—topics like fear, procrastination, excuse making, mastering time, all the way through to the need of being absolutely and consistently authentic. Topics, skills, and habits that can quite simply make or break any sales career.

I chose to concentrate on the concept of habits, since without doubt the most prolific and professional of salespeople have a consistent approach that is quite habitual in nature and ultimately successful. Not only do they have a consistency of approach individually, but there also appears to be a consistency among all professional salespeople—the clues are there when you are curious enough to seek them out. My hope through this book is to illuminate some of the patterns and habits used by these, the most successful of all sales professionals. The Top 1%!

My own style is one of openness and honesty—to share with you what it's really like in sales and give you what you need to succeed. Of course, any short book on sales cannot possibly hope to cover everything you will need in your sales career, no matter how well researched and written. However, I truly believe that the following thirteen key topics are the ones that consistently create the most challenges AND the most opportunities for ALL sales professionals. Also, it's clear to me that all of these topics can be mastered with suitable application applied by the eager student. If you are reading this book now, know you are in exactly the right place at exactly the right time.

Together we will explore the sales challenges you have had, currently encounter, or will face, then develop an understanding that each of these challenges is normal and to be expected. This book will help you create thought processes and supply tools that will allow you to smash these challenges apart—one by one!

So let's begin . . .

THE CONNECTING HABIT

(Aligning with People)

1

The Connection Key

*"Communication—the human connection—is the key to
personal and career success."*
Paul J. Meyer

The basis of all sales (and in fact all marketing) lies in the
ability to CONNECT with a potential buyer. This connection
need is a basic human requirement that resides in every one of
us. It transcends race, creed, nationality, gender, wealth, age, and
social status. It is the starting point that all sales professionals must
master in order to gain the trust and respect necessary to progress,
and ultimately complete a sale. This connection requirement is not
just with prospective customers but also includes partners, internal
support staff, management, and in fact anyone directly or indirectly
involved with you.

The Only Person in the World!

To understand connection better, let's look at a hypothetical
story that includes you being the only person in the world. You
have everything you could possibly need, want, and imagine—
except no access to other people. There are no other people—just
you. You spend your days doing whatever you want, whether it's
driving fast cars or lazing in the sun. But there are no people with
which to share any of the experiences of your day, or your life.
Now, something unexpected happens—you discover the existence

of another human being one day who is so like you in many ways. He is of a similar age, has similar values, similar experiences, and similar hobbies. You simply cannot wait to meet him and start communicating!

What you quickly realize on the first encounter is the other person loves to talk. He, too, thought he was the only person in the world, and now can't wait to share with you all the cool things he has done and all the challenges he has faced. He starts talking and doesn't stop. Then unexpectedly there is a small gap in the monologue, and you decide to jump in. Not to be outdone, you decide to employ the same strategy and start talking quickly, sharing as many of your own unique stories and experiences as possible. This "process" continues, with each party jumping into the conversation at the first sign of a possible break. The communication between both of you continues for hours. Then magically and unexpectedly, just as quickly as the other person appeared, he disappears.

You are left with your own thoughts and your own life again. You start to reflect to see if the experience was as positive and meaningful as you hoped it would be. As you reflect more on what just happened, you realize you gave (and received) lots of information. In fact, lots and lots of information! But yet you feel somewhat empty, somehow disappointed at a deeper level. You soon realize that although there was a significant amount of communication that took place, there was no connection (or connecting) to the other person. You now realize you know a lot about what the other person has done, but not ABOUT the other person. You both failed to connect with each other and missed the golden opportunity to create a basis, a strong foundation, from which all other communication would naturally and effortlessly flow. If only you could get another chance, another opportunity, you would know that *connecting first* is simply the most important thing to do in any new relationship.

It's a simple yet thought-provoking story that highlights the biggest challenge in sales—trying to sell something without first connecting with the other person. Now, I am not saying that if you don't connect well with your prospective customer, a sale cannot be achieved; instead I am strongly suggesting that in today's hypercompetitive business environment, customers have choice. And knowing that choice exists, it's smart and necessary to realize people *like* to buy from people they have a connection with. You lose nothing by trying to make a connection first, and in so doing differentiate yourself from a large percentage of all sales professionals today!

Five Essential Tools for Connection

There are of course many ways to create a connection with someone, whether in your business or personal life. Over time you should become able to draw from a number of tools for creating connection, using the best tool for each circumstance. Know that the tool is important, but the real goal must be to make a solid connection with the other party in the least amount of time. Try these five simple connection tools that my good friend Dinesh Kandanchatha (serial entrepreneur, myVPsales.com) and I wrote about for a recent book we created entitled *The Connection Habit*.

1. The Dual Mind

Arguably the most powerful of the five tools is the inherent ability every human being has of doubling their brainpower in any communication. I learned this principle when I was 21 and on my first presentation skills course. Each person, with their prepared presentation, delivered their "five minutes of fame" in front of a video camera. The video was played back in front of everyone, and feedback duly delivered. My own presentation was pretty good; I knew my topic well, I spoke clearly and with good tone, and my pace was appropriate for the audience. However, I had my back to the audience for the full presentation—oh dear!

The trainer, who had obviously seen this challenge before, told the class everyone has a brain that is even more powerful than we realize. In fact, we should consider using only half our brain for the actual presentation delivery, and the other half should be seated in the audience, giving feedback to the presenter on what the audience sees. After re-recording the video later that afternoon, my lowest score of the day became the highest score of the day—lesson learned!

In defining the *dual mind*, the two roles of the mind were more formally defined: the *actor* (responsible for delivery of the communication/message) and the *observer* (responsible for providing feedback to the actor). When applied to any communication, whether one-on-one or in front of a large audience, the observer senses feedback on what the other people are thinking, perceiving, and doing. The actor then processes this feedback, and the delivery of the communication/message is adjusted accordingly. The ability to perceive what is happening with your audience and make necessary adjustments is one of the greatest skills a sales professional can attain. It allows the ability to sense what the other person needs first, which is to *connect* with you. When this connection has taken place, let the communication begin!

2.   The Three Brains

Research conducted in the 1960s on the brain and its working by the prominent brain researcher Dr. Paul MacLean highlighted the three major centers of the brain. Of course, research has improved dramatically in recent years; however, the concepts he developed are extremely applicable for how we connect with other human beings. He postulated that the brain was actually three brains in one, and he named them the *reptilian brain*, the *mammalian brain*, and the *primate brain*. Each brain has unique characteristics and can be understood by reviewing people's thoughts, intentions, and actions. This approach highlighted three very distinct processing engines inside the brain, with very different approaches and needs.

The *reptilian brain* is the oldest part of the brain and is responsible for what many people understand as the "flight or fight" response. Specifically, it decides in any given situation if a threat is perceived and whether to stay and fight, or to flee away from the danger at hand. The *mammalian brain* is responsible for relationships and the emotional and intellectual subconscious, and is commonly known as the "feeling brain." Lastly, the *primate brain* is responsible for language, abstract thought, consciousness, and imagination, and is known as the "logical brain." Knowing the existence of the *three brains*, a skilled sales professional can perceive what brain is being used at any given point in time and tailor their communication approach accordingly.

If a prospective customer is all hot and bothered, the likelihood is they are using their reptilian brain. If you encounter someone like this, resist all temptations to use your reptilian brain in response. When both reptilian brains are engaged simultaneously, an argument or disagreement will likely ensue, and all logical thought abandoned. Sales professionals should also be able to notice the use of the reptilian brain within themselves in an instant and immediately stop its use! When seen in others, it's wise to first "calm the person down" using both the mammalian and the primate brains' capabilities. I have seen many sales professionals who get drawn into an argument with a customer because one reptilian brain managed to fire up the other reptilian brain! All my experience tells me that there can be no connection created when someone is using their reptilian brain—quite simply, someone wants to fight or wants to run and is certainly not in any frame of mind to connect!

When any type of feeling is discussed or shown, it's likely the output of the mammalian brain. In sales, it's wise to listen carefully to the words being used by a customer. "I feel . . . ," "I need . . . ," and "I worry . . ." are all indicators the emotional brain is being used. When faced with this, using your mammalian brain in response can create empathy and, through this connection. Many sales professionals feel uncomfortable in discussions like this, but it's possibly the fastest way of making a lasting connection with someone.

The last of the *three brains* is what I commonly call the "Mr. Spock" brain—or more formally, the primate brain. It's all about data, facts, evidence, and logic. I am sure even with this brief description you can immediately identify people in your own career who are heavily primate-brain centered. When someone is predominantly this way, it's wise to take a more formal approach for connection and deal in specifics, which will appeal to them. A connection can take place with this approach; however, it takes much more time than using the more empathetic mammalian brain.

Knowing the existence of the *three brains*, and with a little practice, you will be able to spot which one is being used (both in yourself and in others). Having this knowledge and coupling it with some of the basic tips above will give you a head start on many of your peers. The simplicity of this approach is what makes it so powerful for everyday life, including your business life!

3. Assumptionator

The biggest pitfall of almost all communication is the natural tendency of human beings to make assumptions. They are easy to create, become effortlessly habitual, and of course we always believe that our assumptions are correct—that's what makes them so challenging. Also, many a communication gets stilted quickly when assumptions are made but not shared, either by you or the other person. This is a very normal flow within a communication and is often seen as a major cause of disagreements, arguments, and even worse!

I saw this challenge clearly when I was on contract as an interim VP of sales. I entered the meeting room with two highly talented sales directors and the CEO. Within a few minutes, the meeting was in chaos. The CEO was in a heated argument with the sales directors and tempers escalating rapidly. Logic began to disappear quickly, everyone's reptilian brains were activated, and zero progress was being made. I noticed what was happening and went to the large whiteboard and drew a line in the middle, then added five bullet points on each side. I asked the CEO five questions to air his assumptions on the five points I thought were relevant, and then I did the same exercise with the sales directors. When both sets of answers were compared, the tension in the room dissipated immediately. Both sides could see they were in full agreement on three of the five points. With one of the two other remaining points, they agreed to politely disagree with each other since it was not so important, and for the last point, an appropriate action taken to resolve it amicably for both sides.

The hidden assumptions above were killing the conversation and the ability to connect in a meaningful way. Airing assumptions is always the smart choice and, by doing so skillfully, can be used as a way to connect with other people. It's also one of the best tools to use to stop getting yourself, and other people, into hot water!

4. Storyteller

There is an old saying I love which reads, "The world loves a good storyteller." Throughout time, stories have been used to engage, train, coach, mentor, and entertain people. We are all hardwired to tell stories (we can all tell stories!), and also to vividly remember them. Stories can be short, medium, or long in length and be based on fact or fiction. They can be used in both one-on-one communication and with large audiences. A good story will always engage the other person when told with authenticity and skill. As an example, everyone will remember from their childhood a memorable story told to them by their parents or teachers, a great novel they have read in their youth, and also their favorite film seen as an adult. All are stories, and no matter how complex they might be, we still remember the main story lines and characters since they touched us in some meaningful ways.

And so it is with connection; sharing a well-told and timely story can be a way for the other person to feel connected with you. Whether you are sharing something in common (like discussing your old school or university) or something new (like the latest adventures of your favorite sports team), stories are among the fastest ways of developing great connection. They tend to be informal, help break the ice in a new relationship, and highlight some sort of commonality in thinking between both parties. Skilled sales professionals know the full power of storytelling to make an initial connection, and know that when used wisely, can lead to the development of even closer connection over time.

5. Silencer

Without doubt one of the hardest skills to develop for a professional salesperson is active listening. The *silencer* is effectively a mental trigger for you to remember to stay quiet and actively listen to the other person. In fact, it should also be coupled with the ability to ask wise and timely questions. Additionally, silence can be used by both parties to allow some much-needed *soak time*, or *thinking time*. For example, some musicians believe the most beautiful music created is not in the delivery of the notes but by the proper spacing of silence between them. This is wise indeed and helps us realize that silence is necessary in any meaningful communication.

When creating an initial connection with someone, silence is a way to show that you are not overbearing, that you are an active listener, and that you are interested in the other person. Quite simply, sales professionals should master the habit of silence both at the initial connection stage and throughout the life of the relationship. And, of course, it must become an available tool to be used when future situations warrant it.

I recall using silence effectively during an initial meeting with a new prospective customer. After a few brief sentences of introduction, I asked him how his day was so far. He replied by telling me a story of his morning, which had been full of supplier challenges. Although it would have been easy for me to jump in at any point and start suggesting ways that I could help, including my belief that none of these horror stories would have happened if he chose to give my company business, I sat quietly and listened instead. The quieter I was, the more he talked. At the end of what seemed like a long time, he said to me, "Thanks! I feel a lot better now." I smiled, and an immediate connection was made, not to mention the fact I had gained lots of great information about my competitors, how they were failing in this account, and what was really important to this particular procurement manager!

As a final thought for this chapter, pay heed to the sage advice contained in this quote, highlighting why learning to make a connection is so vitally important in all sales activities:

"Internalize the Golden Rule of sales that says: All things being equal, people will do business with, and refer business to, those people they know, like and trust."
Bob Burg

Summary

1. Customers prefer to buy from people they have a connection with. It's not impossible to sell without a connection, but you are immediately disadvantaged in comparison to those who choose connection first.
2. Making a connection happens differently for different people—learn the five essential tools for connection until you can instinctively and automatically use the right tool at the right time.
3. Connection is extremely important to kick-start a relationship, but is equally important to maintain throughout the entire relationship. Invest the time to connect during every interaction.

Remember Only This

"Choose to CONNECT first!"

2

Building Teamwork

*"Teamwork is so important that it is virtually impossible
for you to reach the heights of your capabilities or make the
money that you want without becoming very good at it."*
Brian Tracey

Sales is a function that involves reaching out, connecting,
meeting and following up with people every single day.
In many instances, it's considered to be a solitary job, one that
requires great steel and determination to keep motivation high
and energy at its peak. However, most sales professionals have
realized the significant benefits of teaming with others to help in
the achievement of their goals.

Teamwork can be created both internally and externally.
Internally it can be with other members of your sales team or
members of the wider company who can get involved in helping
find the optimal customer solution. Externally, it can be with
partners or an extended sales organization that provide additional
ideas and effort to push things forward. Last, but certainly not least,
teamwork can happen directly with the customer. When the sales
professional and the customer come together in a spirit of *doing
the right things at the right time* for the benefit of all parties, real
sales magic can be created! All sales professionals should strive to
develop teamwork through all three options above and thus create
extended teams that provide both additional insight and higher
likelihood of sales success.

I recall an event in my sales career when I was working for a large semiconductor company in the United States. During the weekly sales call that included all worldwide regions, it became clear a certain large competitor was methodically targeting our customer base. Each regional sales director had roughly the same story—their big customers were being aggressively approached by our competitor and asked directly what it would take to "design us out"! Some of the directors had some good ideas on what could be done locally, but what took place next was simply an example of decisive strategy, immediate action, and a show of worldwide coordination and teamwork.

The CEO asked the Vice President of sales to host a "war room." It consisted of taking over a conference room and using it to host a thirty minute meeting each morning at 8:00 a.m. sharp, to discuss short-term strategies and implement urgent actions. An elite team was pulled together, including representatives from sales, marketing, and engineering. Their goal was to stop the threat of the competitor in the best and fastest possible way. They met daily, listened to challenges, removed roadblocks, took actions, and ultimately reacted superfast with a barrage of positive actions and outcomes that neutralized the competitive threat. Quite simply, incredible teamwork yielding output that a single sales professional could never have dreamed of.

What Exactly is Teamwork?

There is an old saying that states, "Nothing worthwhile was ever accomplished by someone alone!" And so it is with teamwork. When given the option of working alone or working as an integral part of a team—and potentially one that you have created yourself—wisdom suggests "going it together." Teamwork is where a group of people is brought together willingly, around a common challenge shared by all, to create a solution beneficial to all. How much work, what role, and what accountability you have in the team are all key elements that must be discussed and agreed upon by all.

Clarity really is the name of the game with teams and teamwork. Everyone should expect direct access to everyone else, keep and be kept informed of challenges, key decisions, and progress, and ultimately feel that they are a valued and respected member. Without doubt the output of a highly focused team will, in almost all instances, far outperform the output of a highly motivated individual. A team-based approach can bring opportunities for increased levels of creativity, smarter problem-solving, and group motivation that can boost morale at almost any time. Teaming and teamwork really is the smart choice!

Why is Teamwork Required?

Today, sales professionals face competitive challenges that appear to be constantly increasing. Even compared with only a few years ago, more information and detail are freely available on the Internet, joint partnerships are becoming more in vogue, and large companies as well as nimble small companies have access to great evolving technologies. In addition, the smart companies are realizing the relationship developed with a customer is always stronger when there are multiple touch points company-to-company. Whether referring to executive, technical or customer service relationships, the higher the number of touch points, the deeper the relationship can be. With so many possible touch points in a company, it makes sense for the sales professional to be the common point of contact internally for coordinating customer activities, and ensuring everyone is kept in the loop.

In today's hypercompetitive business environment, many sales challenges can be quite complex, especially if your product or service is by its very nature complex to begin with. Teaming can help brainstorm highly creative solutions, really prize out problem definition and solutions, and also provide an overall competitive edge when done successfully. It takes great wisdom to know when to tackle something yourself, normally for the sake of expediency, and when to create and motivate a team to help. The simple reality is, the more teamwork that is created, managed well, and output generated, the more success a sales professional can have within the account. Now, teamwork of course is not relevant to every opportunity or challenge within a customer, but it should be considered as often as possible due to the significant benefits with this approach.

From my standpoint, it's clear the best teams are always created when there are one or more customers involved. The dynamics of the team change—and normally for the better—the professionalism often increases, and there is a real feeling the team is doing something fundamentally important; something truly worthwhile for the customer. Oftentimes sales professionals miss the opportunity of suggesting a joint team with the customer, and you can be sure that if your competitor has one in place and you don't, you will be heavily disadvantaged from the outset. Become even more competitive and learn to team with your customers!

What Are the Benefits of Teamwork?

We have mentioned some of the benefits earlier regarding teamwork. However, there are many more possible when done correctly. The other manifestation of great teamwork is the desire to do more of it—in essence, success breeding success. Review these ten teamwork benefits and see if you can add a few more from your own experiences:

1. Eliminates competition earlier.
2. Shows a strong up-front customer commitment.
3. Brings in a fun, competitive team spirit.
4. Aids internal communication and coordination.
5. Builds your reputation as a team player.
6. Generates better, and more, ideas.
7. Delivers faster throughput of actions.
8. Delegates actions to the best people for the job.
9. Shows the customer the depth of your internal support team.
10. Hones your management and teamwork skills.

At the outset, remember to review if creating a team is the best option, and if it is, then do so as quickly and as efficiently as possible. Aligning the team with a common vision of output, and showing them clearly what's in it for them and others, will help create both a stronger team and one that will ultimately be more successful.

Other Options to Teamwork

As a sales professional, you will likely have developed a wide range of options to solve a challenge. The more options or tools in your tool kit, the better. As you gain experience, continue to find new and innovative ways to solve problems, while at the same time adding these skills or tools to your available future options. One of the key differentiators in moving into a sales management role, and potentially even a sales executive role, is the ability to identify challenges and then come up with options to solve them, using the right tool for the job, at exactly the right time. Consider watching and learning from your own sales leaders and see how they are being successful and the approaches they are taking. Here are some other alternative methods to consider:

1. **Go it alone:** Many actions are best handled alone, and quickly. Whenever the action is within your scope of experience and expertise, this approach is normally best. However, always do a quick check at this stage and consider if a teaming approach could possibly yield a higher-quality output as viewed through the eyes of the customer.

2. **Delegate responsibility:** This is a wise option especially when there are a large number of actions to complete. Having the maturity to seek help, and the professionalism to share positive outcomes, will all but guarantee you long-term and consistent support.

3. **Let the customer direct you:** Oftentimes a customer may have better or more information than you, the supplier (or

service provider). Asking the customer what is the preferred solution for them can be the smart option, especially when you believe that the output is within your control to implement. Choose this option wisely, and always consider it, since successfully implementing it can build fast connection with most customers.

4. **Create an internal team:** This makes sense whenever the actions are of a confidential nature, potentially related to a new device or technology, and also when there is specific and needed expertise required that you know resides within your company.

5. **Create an external team:** This option can be valuable when working with an extended, or external, sales organization, like reps or distributors. There may be an option to work closely with partners who are in some way involved; it could be a value-added reseller who adds incremental functionality or usability to your offering, or provides an overall solution that is simply more compelling than your stand-alone one. It is wise to consider this option whenever possible, since its certainly possible your competition will be looking into this closely. Choose your partners well since they, by default, will become part of your offering and your team!

6. **Create a customer-centered team:** Without doubt this option can yield the most leverage. When you work closely with a customer in the spirit of trust, openness, and teamwork, you can really engage and involve them. It shows a willingness to listen and to partner. At this stage, be careful of building up expectations that ultimately cannot be fulfilled. Nonetheless, I have often seen concessions being positively made by both sides when a partnership like this is created. It's a bit more work and takes more time to manage, but the results can be fantastic.

7. **Procrastinate:** If you really think this is a viable option, then immediately read chapter 5!

Note that the "go it alone" option is the one most inexperienced salespeople take, since they believe it will be both faster and more efficient. As experience develops, the professional salesperson soon realizes the "extra" up-front effort to implement some of the other options above can yield far superior results, bond a team together to create output more than the sum of the individual parts, and ultimately become a winning proposition. Try developing each of the options above one by one, taking the necessary time to become proficient in each, before moving on to learning and implementing the next one. Once you have successfully implemented them all, you will have an extensive tool kit to choose from, and your likelihood of incremental and future success will have increased significantly!

One of the best examples of teamwork I have been directly part of is related to the winning of large customer opportunities. When I was Vice President of sales and responsible for winning these multimillion-dollar opportunities, I decided to implement an opportunity management system called Large Account Management (LAMP) also commonly known as Blue Sheets from Miller Heiman Inc. (www.millerheiman.com). This process was used to do a deep-dive into large opportunities and through a structured and questioning approach ensure there were no gaps in our offering. Each sales director was required to complete their own Blue Sheet, but the real magic happened when there was a sales team review. Initially we started by having the sales directors and myself review each Blue Sheet in a collaborative team environment. This yielded lots of new ideas, great insight, and ultimately made our position stronger at each of the accounts. Then, the CEO asked me if he and key members of the executive team could also be involved in these reviews. Initially I was hesitant, but we tried it to see if anything good would come from it. Incredibly even more ideas poured in, great questions identified, and solutions that were simply outside the scope of the sales team operating alone were generated. This was a great learning experience for me—to cast the teamwork net even wider for the most important, must-win opportunities.

Consider trying this approach in your own company since I have used it numerous times myself in other sales environments, and also coached a lot of senior sales professionals as to its obvious and practical merits.

Challenges to Building Teamwork

It's clear that building teamwork can on occasion be challenging. As they say, "Not everything in the garden is rosy all the time!" It's the same with knowing when best to create a team, how to set goals for them, how to manage them, and ultimately how to successfully disband them. Without doubt the biggest challenge you will face in creating a team is the recruiting of new team members who say, "Why me?". Most people, whether internal or external to your company, have busy jobs and a set of priorities that you may or, more likely, may not know well. Your job is to identify the right people to join the team and explain the benefits to them in such a way they'll choose to allocate some of their precious time to this worthwhile endeavor. I have found the following simple process can help create, and subsequently galvanize, a new team together:

1. **Choose great team members:** This can often be the most challenging aspect of this process, since it's your responsibility to identify key members who'll bring knowledge, expertise, and determination to the group. They must ideally be team players themselves and be clear on the goals and outcomes required.

2. **Explain the value proposition(s) through their eyes:** Each team member will be happy to join and actively participate once they know what the benefit is for them personally. Of course, they will also want to know in detail what the goals and outcomes are for the whole team, and in

particular for you, since you are the one organizing it in the first place. Remember that a value proposition here is of the most benefit when delivered through the eyes of the future team members. Make it personal for them, and the chances of them joining will go up exponentially!

3. **Bring the team together regularly:** Naturally the team must be brought together at the beginning to align everyone on goals, outcomes, and the expected challenges they will undoubtedly encounter along the way. Remember to bring them back together regularly to check in with progress, align on communication and status, and provide much needed customer feedback to ensure everything is on track. Additionally, a well-performing team can brainstorm solutions to problems much better than any single individual can.

4. **Encourage equal and active participation:** As you convey the value propositions individually to team members, some people may be more excited than others and be willing to do more. This is great, but also remember to try and involve all participants equally, if possible. The dynamics and output always appear to be stronger when there is an equal sharing of the workload.

5. **Continually motivate the team:** As the team leader, it's your responsibility to orchestrate the overall success of the team. Depending on how long the team has been in existence, it makes sense to keep them highly motivated, since by doing so it will bring better and more rapid results. This will entail extra effort on your part, but will be well worth the additional investment.

6. **Disband the team on successful completion:** It's important to know when the team should be disbanded. Often they stay together longer than they should, suffer

from a dissipation of energy and excitement, and begin to naturally break apart. Instead, close out the team with a celebration proportionate to the success achieved. Even though all of the key outcomes may not have been realized exactly as planned, pick the successes and celebrate them. This will help galvanize everyone and make it easier the next time you have to solicit their help.

Essential Sales Skills to Build Teamwork

As you mature in your sales role, you will undoubtedly develop skills and knowledge on how best to create and motivate teams successfully. If you think of them in a similar light as you would a customer, you will quickly see the skills are exactly the same as those required in your customer interactions. Don't try and do anything too fancy, but instead stick to the basics and doing them well. They include the ability to make a connection and keep it, the ethical delivery of value propositions that appeal to the team members individually and collectively, the ability to communicate in a timely manner, the tenacity to work through problems as they arise, and the wisdom to know that no matter what the outcome, a celebration of some sort is in order. Stick with these basics and build winning teams that dramatically accelerate your sales outcomes and ultimately your sales success.

> *"When you start out in a team, you have to get the teamwork going and then you get something back."*
> **Michael Schumacher**

Summary

1. Teamwork is an action-centered approach, which should be considered frequently to allow faster completion and higher-quality output.

2. Teamwork takes extra effort compared to other options, but when used wisely, yields an output far greater than any individual could ever achieve.
3. Consider recruiting the customer to your team as often as practical, since in so doing you create a stronger connection, gain greater insight, and potentially generate a competitive and winning advantage.

Remember Only This

"Teamwork is about going it TOGETHER!"

THE ELIMINATING HABIT

(Crushing Unwanted Traits)

3

Removing Fears

"When you do what you fear most, then you can do anything."
Stephen Richards

There's an old story about a man who had a fear of being followed. He would regularly and periodically see a shadow behind him. After looking for clues, he realized that he would get some respite, but only at certain times of the day. When the sun was out, he knew he was being followed—he could see the shadow. When the evening darkness began to fall, again he would see the shadow. It got so bad that he believed he was also being followed in his own home—but not until the houselights were on in the evening! It seems like a crazy story to think that his shadow was in fact someone different from himself, someone who was following him. In many ways he was crazy, but in many ways he was right—a shadow was following him. And so it is with fear!

Discovering What Fear Really Is

Fear belongs to the person who allows it into their daily life. Fear is your amazing imagination working at full power, to transport you magically into the future, and somehow gain predictive powers that let you know what will happen to you. The reality is that most people have fears, and some have fears so powerful that they shape their achievements, or lack thereof, for their entire lives. Fear has a clear and direct correlation with action, or more specifically inaction. So let's look a bit deeper at what materializes when fear raises its ugly self to you.

Normally something happens—an event, a catalyst—that "forces" you to think about what will then occur. Your mind once exposed to the catalyst has a need to fill the subsequent void created, the void of uncertainty. It is clear the mind is a great processing engine with literally billions of neurons firing constantly, and your catalyst has just given them a big and supposedly immediate task— foretell the future and do it right now! Your mind is convinced the outcome is important and starts "thinking" more about it. At this point your heartbeat will increase, your blood pressure will increase, your breathing increases, your senses become more active, and you feel more alert. This feeling is the clear start of the "fight or flight" mechanism activated by the reptilian brain. Interestingly, the vast majority of situations we face in the modern world today do not require us to fight for our life or flee to preserve it, but the reptilian brain does not know that! Instead it gets you prepared for fast and immediate action.

Now, at this point something really unusual happens in the majority of people. Instead of taking the immediate action suggested by the reptilian brain, most times there will be no one "to fight" and nowhere "to flee." However, the mind is still firing, now even quicker, the body reacting accordingly, and no subsequent action being taken! What's happening with this mind-storm that has just materialized in an instant? The energy needs to be consumed somewhere, so it begins to feed on itself. The fear starts to feed on fear and build up intensity. Still no action, just a racing pulse, and racing thoughts—all about future and unknown events. You can sense now that you are getting uptight, likely nervous, and certainly concerned about some perceived future event or situation. Your mind is now so alert thinking at such a rapid rate that you feel the need to think even more about the fear and really gain clarity around the expected future and its consequences. This cycle continues, gaining momentum, seemingly unstoppable. But still no action!

At this point if you were to stop and analyze the thoughts you are having within this mind-storm, do you think they would be predominantly positive or negative in nature? If it's fear you are feeling, then they are more than likely negative thoughts, based on a set of actions that your mind has chosen to fabricate, whose outcome is anything but positive and causes you genuine worry, anxiety, and inaction. It seems almost crazy that the reptilian brain is screaming for action (fight or flight), and the modern professional salesperson is caught in the quagmire of inaction! This is the onset of negative, debilitating fear and subsequent stress, and is without doubt the major cause of poor sales performance all around the globe! Wow!

On reflection, a few questions that may immediately come to mind are:

1. Why does my mind fire up so quickly and have an immediate need to try and predict the future?
2. Are my fears unique only to me?
3. Why do I have predominantly negative thoughts and not positive ones?
4. Why does this reaction cause even more debilitating negative thoughts?
5. Why do I not take positive, affirmative action immediately to stem the mind-storm?
6. Why have I done this all my life without having solved it, since it happens so frequently?
7. Is it possible to remove my fears permanently?
8. Am I really going crazy?

I should probably help you answer question 8 immediately and say that it's highly unlikely! The fears we all have, and our normal mental, physical, and emotional reactions to them are in fact well understood. It's fair to say that all human beings have faced their own fears (and subsequent reactions to them) at one time of their lives or another—in the history of mankind, that's over 100 billion people! So whatever you do now, don't worry about it! The good news is it's a solvable challenge, and fears and their debilitating outcomes can be dramatically reduced or in some cases eradicated entirely by the application of the right thought processes. Indeed there are many systems available today that have been created by wise people who have experienced these challenges firsthand. In fact the ideas below to manage your own fears are based on the fact that I was so heavily plagued by debilitating fears myself!

The Fear-Accepting Program

As I worked through my own vivid set of daily fears, especially the ones related to prospecting, networking, and fighting for new business, I realized that I was trying to solve everything all at the same time—I was looking for the magic blue pill that if taken would immediately solve everything! Well, we all know that is not possible, so I decided to break the challenge down into a few simple steps—namely, beginning to accept my fears and then, once mastered, beginning to eradicate them.

What is interesting to note is that when the mind-storm event or catalyst happens, your mind reacts so quickly that oftentimes it's difficult to catch it in this action. However, it can be done and requires a little use of muscle memory. As you read this, and hopefully it's resonating with you, you will be sowing the seeds of knowledge in your mind. Once there, they will be locked in forever—that's the good news. Now the question is how do you activate that knowledge at the right time, as the fear and subsequent mind-storm begin to brew. Fortunately, the concepts are simple and just require a little, but consistent, practice before they become automatic.

(a) Before the Mind-Storm

Most fears ultimately predict "big" negative outcomes in my experience. To counteract this before the mind-storm starts, develop a clear vision for the important goals of your life, making them exactly what you truly want to happen. For example, if you want to earn $100,000 this year, clearly add that to your personal vision and think positively and regularly about it. Write it down, dream about it, imagine it, and even try to feel what it will be like when you achieve this goal. Review it every day and ask yourself if you are taking the right and necessary actions to achieve it. Take quiet time when it's available and think positively about your goal. This activates the *Law of Attraction* and the subsequent coincidences and synchronicities that will begin to materialize for you. Commit to staying positive and thinking positively. The more you do this, the more you are training your muscle memory to positive actions and outcomes—the opposite forces of fear!

(b) During the Mind-Storm

With a little practice, skill, and time, you will be able to recognize and catch the fear as it materializes in your mind. As the fear arises (as it probably will), choose not to be worried about it. Instead let the fear enter your mind, and then start to become curious about it. Think about the fear-thought. Ask yourself why the fear-thought has come at this time. Ask yourself to really clarify what the fear-thought is with as much clarity as you can. Spend a few moments wrestling with the thought in your mind trying to seek more clarity on what it's really saying. Again, resist reacting to it. This is a key step since it's a way of keeping the mind active by thinking about a positive challenge. Accept the fear-thought, don't try at this stage to quash it, and instead welcome this time to proactively think about it. You will quickly find that your reactions are significantly different this time around. The mind-storm will quickly stop, and your curiosity (which is amazingly powerful) will begin working on asking clarifying questions. Your heartbeat, blood pressure, and breathing will all quickly return to normal, and you will feel the negative energy and "uncontrollability" of the fear-thought dissipate. The more you practice this, the more you will be able to catch yourself in real time and the more curious you will become. You are now taking back control of your fears!

(c) After the Mind-Storm

When calmness prevails, as it always seems to do, ask yourself if there is anything you noticed as the fears arose and how you chose to handle them. Then ask, did it create any ideas for suitable actions you might undertake? When a fear-thought arises, and you handle it through acceptance, there is always a learning and an action to be found, if you only take the time to find them. This time for personal reflection is one of the toughest things to do in our modern, busy lives, but by making the time—even if it's a short stop at a coffee shop, some quiet driving time, or when walking the dog—it will be time well spent. Realize clearly that the vast majority of fears and their predicted outcomes simply never materialize!

The Fear-Removing Program

All professional salespeople have an innate ability to take action. They also have the ability to repeat things that are successful and to reap and appreciate the benefits of those successes. By diligently practicing the *Fear-Accepting Program*, you will begin to inherently see success in managing and accepting your fears. Your confidence will grow, you will see that fears as they arise can be managed appropriately, and the output becomes a state of calmness; through this, the creation of positive ideas and actions will get kick-started. This is a big step forward—actually a huge step forward. Congratulations!

To remove fears now that you have learned the skill to accept them, you simply have to create a new mind trigger. Again the opportunity lies in catching the superfast, reactionary reptilian brain at the earliest possible stage. In the *Fear-Accepting Program*, the first stage was to catch the reptilian brain starting to create the mind-storm, then choosing to accept it and ultimately becoming curious about it. Now you can accelerate things dramatically by catching the reptilian brain creating the fear-thought at the outset, then choosing to activate your new mental trigger to say,

"STOP!" The very moment this happens, choose NOT TO DEVELOP the fear-thought. Instead play back something positive related to your personal vision statement. You have immediately stopped the negative thought and replaced it with a positive one. Again, it takes time, patience, and practice to master this. However, it can be mastered, and the corresponding results can be simply spectacular. Try it, stick with it, and then reap the significant rewards of your efforts. Remember to keep choosing this practice, and soon it will become so automatic you won't even realize you're doing it—the beginnings of true sales habit mastery!

The Most Common Sales Fears

Realizing that all fears are not in any way unique—and in the world of sales, almost all fears are in fact common—I have listed some examples below to illustrate this point. What matters most is you can now begin to understand you are not unique in this respect, other people have or have had these fears, and that all of them can be accepted and removed, thus causing an explosion of positive energy and action to rapidly accelerate your sales success.

1. I will get fired.
2. People will think I am not good enough.
3. I will not hit my budget this year.
4. I will not earn as much as I want or need.
5. I will need to find a new job.
6. I won't be able to win this customer.
7. The competition is too tough.
8. I will not get promoted.
9. I am not as good as I think I am.
10. The business environment is getting tougher every day.
11. I will go bankrupt.
12. My peer group is too smart and experienced.
13. I won't be able to get the price I need.
14. People will never call me back.
15. I won't hit all my objectives this year.

16. I won't be able to recover in time.
17. I am going to lose this business now.
18. I won't be able to find new customers.
19. I won't be able to book that meeting.
20. People won't like me.

As a matter of interest, and maybe fun, why not take a few minutes and create your own list. Shoot for at least ten items and try and get to twenty of your most common fears related to being in sales. Once you generate the list, spend some time over the coming weeks simply reviewing it and see what thoughts come up. These fears are likely to be pretty consistent and, if not addressed using the two programs above, will likely stay with you and embed themselves even deeper into your psyche. So be bold and take that first positive step of implementing the *Fear-Accepting Program*!

Even though I have been in sales and marketing roles for 28 years, and having been very successful in my career, I realized that I still suffered basic debilitating fears. For me it was always related to prospecting and networking and meeting people for the very first time. I so wanted them to really like me, to know I was a good guy, and that they should consider doing business with me. My fears materialized in lots of different ways—from choosing not to make timely prospecting calls, not attending networking events, all the way to using e-mail as much as possible instead of the phone. I realized through lots of self-reflection that my challenge was not other people but was in fact myself. As I started to concentrate on working on myself and accepting and being curious about my own fears, and then ultimately catching them early enough to eradicate them, I was left with positive thoughts, creative actions to take, and a renewed belief in my ability to achieve my personal vision. Of course as that happened, I magically began to hit and actually exceed all my sales goals! I then quickly realized the very direct correlation between removing fears from my mind and achieving the sales success I always desired in life!

*"Courage is never to let your actions be influenced
by your fears."*
Arthur Koestler

Summary

1. Fears are normal human emotions; start by recognizing and accepting them in real time, then slowly building up to eradicating them.
2. Fears are the biggest catalyst of inaction in a professional salesperson; removing them frees up huge amounts of positive energy that can be applied to growing your business.
3. Removing fears and benefiting from this output is the biggest determinant of sales success bar none.

Remember Only This

"Conquer your fears—it's in you to do so now!"

4

Extinguishing Excuses

"Don't make excuses and don't talk about it. Do it."
Melvyn Douglas

As a seasoned, results-focused coach for sales professionals, business owners, and executives, I come across what I lovingly call *The Book of Excuses* on a daily basis. I have to tell you it's a long book, containing many ways to make excuses and a list of great ones that can be used—and there does not appear to be any copyrights on these excuses! It covers almost every situation imaginable and somehow convinces readers that everything is unique and just for them! The excuses can be simple or complex, technical or nontechnical, highly practical or out of this world. It advises on how best to use excuses, whether it be matter-of-fact or emotional, data-driven or concept-oriented, tried-and-true or something uniquely interesting. With regular practice, and a bit of trial and error, most people can become masters of making the excuse! But why?

There seems to be something in the human psyche that when confronted by a challenge, a task, or anything that remotely feels tough, our minds automatically jump to making excuses. It seems to be a reaction rather than conscious thought and is often unknown to the speaker. We are then convinced by our own excuses and in fact seek to defend our position with gusto. All the while our mind is telling us we are still a good person even though we are effectively in a state of closed negativity. So can anything be done about this natural human reaction, and is it worth the effort to resolve for us personally, our organizations, and ultimately for our customers?

What Exactly Are Excuses?

An excuse is simply where you seek to justify or defend a position or opinion you have, which ultimately STOPS you from taking action—simply put it's an action stopper! But interestingly it is not necessarily an energy-reducer or energy-stopper, since many people expend huge amounts of energy defending their excuse position rather than actually "just doing the action." It's a strange phenomenon, but one that is prevalent both in business and in life.

Excuses can come in many forms, often disguised as something else, but excuses nonetheless. In life as in sales, I have seen excuses masquerading as rational argument (logical reasons why I am not going to do the action), heightened emotions (I am sharing and empathizing with you, but I am not going to do the action), all the way through to the illogical reptilian-brain-generated reaction (I am not thinking about it; just telling you that I am not going to the do the action since I feel threatened in some way). Excuses can be delivered slowly or quickly, with a simple yes or no, with an extravagant explanation, by the spoken word, by any of our modern communication accessories, and matter-of-factly or with emotion. They can be repeated, built on, changed, manipulated, emphasized, relayed, and in fact simply energized by even more thinking and defending of your non-action position. Wow!

Why Do We Make Excuses?

One of the key lessons in sales is to get to the bottom of why we, and others, are continually making excuses. It seems to be a pandemic that is rampant in every individual, company, and country across the world. So it makes sense to get to the bottom of why people make excuses since this can ultimately be a guide to their driving force, and their true intentions. Of course many people know their true intentions when they make an excuse, but others will have reasons that are buried deep beneath their surface, and it takes great sales skill to patiently unearth them. The professional salesperson will always strive to identify these deeper reasons, since knowing them gives great power of understanding, the subsequent ability to remove obstacles ethically, and ultimately increases their sales performance.

Someone once said that "excuses are like egos, everyone has one, they are difficult to control, and can feed quickly on one another." It's a fair description and one that highlights excuse making is part of the deep human psyche. I am not sure exactly where excuses come from, whether it's something embedded into our cells or is something that we develop as children, then further developed in adolescence and later as adults. One thing however is clear, as we get older, our ability and skill at being able to make excuses increases dramatically. It is also clear that people develop standard excuses for different situations. My favorites, which I often use myself, are "I don't have the time," "I am too tired," and "It won't work—trust me." All little automatic triggers that somehow I believe will protect me either from making an effort, tackling the action, protecting myself in some way, or maybe even feeling the success of the action completion. In these situations, I often respond so quickly that it's evident I have reacted rather than thought about my response.

Of course many people can point to laziness, intransigence, ignorance, or other negative traits as the source of excuse making, and in some cases this is correct. But yet there are still underlying reasons why these traits yield the excuse-rich response. Again in sales, try playing the detective to uncover the underlying motivations of these excuses, since this knowledge is definitely considered powerful, if used appropriately.

Why Do We Continue to Make Excuses?

As a former Vice President of sales for a busy company, I often found myself having a queue of people outside my office. I likened it to a busy General Practitioners Office waiting to see patients.

Each patient would come in and express their own "problem of the day," wait patiently, and expect me to provide medication (a solution). I would ask them diligently why they had not solved their problem by themselves. After a while I realized everyone was making excuses, reading from their own personal and private copy of *The Book of Excuses*! I continued with this routine for years and felt very important. I knew the organization needed me! Then one day I awoke and realized I truly had great staff and had unconsciously trained them not to think—wow! It was time for a change. I created a simple-to-implement, efficient process that changed my entire management style, positively empowered my staff, and subsequently took a considerable amount of stress off me. It also freed up a significant amount of my time. This process is applicable for anyone who has inadvertently developed the bad habit of excuse making. Try this five-step, easy-to-implement process in a sales situation today and be curious about the results you will achieve (beware that it really works!):

1. **Inform** the person to stop using negatively charged words like *problem* and *issue*, and instead use positively charged and motivational words like *challenge* and *opportunity*: "Let's resolve this challenge" or "Let's capitalize on this opportunity."

2. **Encourage** them to spend quality time on their own to more fully understand what the issue is, so they can communicate it more effectively.

3. **Ask** them to bring at least one solution to the "challenge" and be able to explain why it's a credible solution.

4. **Alert** them that you will pro-actively ask questions about the challenge and their solution in equal measure.

5. **Resist** giving them the answer (your preferred answer), and instead choose to use it as a way to discover different possible solutions jointly.

What's interesting is that the five-step process can be applied just as effectively to you. When you take the time to think and be curious, you will discover much about yourself, your fears, your motivations, and ultimately what it takes to reduce excuse making, and instead TAKE ACTION!

With a consistent approach, you will begin to see yourself and others becoming more positive, more empowered, and with a stronger can-do attitude.

My Top Ten Sales Excuses

Excuses come in all shapes and sizes, and some of the best ones I have heard over the years have stuck with me. Some are serious, some funny, but all are action stoppers. Enjoy the list below, but as you read and reflect on them, see if you have used them or ones like them in the past. Also, see if you can add a few more of your own personal favorites.

1. I got caught in traffic.
2. My phone is having problems.
3. My e-mail crashed—again.
4. I was sick.
5. I missed the plane.
6. I am too busy.
7. I'll do it later.
8. Let me think about it.
9. I'll get back to you.
10. It's not my responsibility.

Lastly, if you don't have the latest copy of *The Book of Excuses*, please don't ask me—I would only say, "I don't have a copy" and have to make up an excuse! Now that would be on page 372!

Makers and Receivers of Excuses

When suitably tuned into hearing excuses, you will quickly realize there are both excuse makers and excuse receivers. The excuse makers deliver the excuses, and the excuse receivers internalize them and subsequently decide on a course of action. Noteworthy, is that excuse making is one of the great causes (catalysts) for arguments and misunderstandings, and the excuse receiver can dramatically change their own reactions (and actions) depending on whether information is delivered as an excuse, or as a challenge. With this knowledge, the professional salesperson is now armed with the ability to stop personally making excuses and instead, by turning them inside out, choose to reframe them as challenges. This is also a worthwhile technique when another party delivers an excuse to you.

The ability to "tune into" excuses is itself a huge skill. If you want to enable a short real-life test of how many excuses you come across in a typical business day as a sales professional, make a note of every excuse you hear—simply mark it in a notebook or an app in your smart phone. When you review the total at the end of the day, I think you might be quite surprised!

Stopping Excuses From Happening

To illustrate this point, let's review a story from my past that has stayed with me, and for good reason:

In my early career, my first promotion was an early one. The new, higher-expectation role was challenging, and there seemed to be incredible demands on my time. It appeared that no matter what I did, there was always something more to do, another opportunity to win, another fire to put out. As the pressure intensified, I recall a strong conversation I had with my boss at the time when he handed me yet another "big task." I fired a whole bunch of excuses at him in rapid succession, all of which I was totally bought into, and told him that it was impossible for me to take on this task. He sat quietly and listened, then asked me, "Do you think it is important?"

I said, "Of course it's important!"

At this, he (again calmly) said to me, "Joe if it's important, then make time!" For a long period (in fact, many years), I did not understand the sage wisdom he had just imparted. In essence the message was if it's a high-enough priority, then it's more important than your lower priorities, so make the time for it. That was the lesson, simple as it was. However, I also suspect embedded in his words were "and stop making excuses!"

Options to Excuse Making

Now, excuses as we all know can build on one another, so it is especially important to stop them by identifying approaches that can be used consistently. Instead choose to encourage creative brainstorming, positive problem-solving, and ultimately exceptional solution-creating. Consider some of these simple and effective tips that I use frequently:

1. **Think before you talk:** Ask the excuse maker to coat-check their reptilian brain—the part of the brain that responds but does not think. Also remember to buy an extra second of thought by taking a breath before you respond—it sounds simple but it really helps!

2. **Ask clarification questions:** Resist the urge to jump in with what you think is the perfect solution. Instead choose to ask more questions and explore individual topics with more rigor. Develop lines of discussion since the best solution is not always immediately evident until explored more deeply.

3. **One problem, one solution:** Consider asking the other person to add one solution for every excuse they identify. You will likely collect a lot of possible solutions that may prove useful later.

4. **"Man on the moon" check:** Stop people from being discouraged with perceived or real problems and their subsequent excuses. Often placing the problem in perspective can kick-start solution finding. My own favorite is the saying "They sent a man to the moon you know—now that was really hard!"

5. **Outcome visioning:** When individual discussions or meetings are getting bogged down, try lifting everyone's spirits by sharing your vision of what the success outcome could look like. Oftentimes aligning on the outcome in enough detail can create sparks of creativity and convince people to positively strive for solutions, thus not adding even more problems and excuses to the mix.

6. **Challenge assumptions:** Someone once said assumptions were the archenemy of creating good lasting solutions. Encourage everyone to actively uncover and discuss assumptions. Through these discussions, alignment can happen quickly, and often solutions become evident when assumptions are aired, discussed, and resolved.

Consider having some fun by creating your own personal, department, or company *Book of Excuses*. You will quickly find some real gems that will make you laugh. When you make an excuse, just pinch yourself (yes, pinch yourself—it works as a reminder for your conscious and subconscious mind). During internal meetings, set a bell off every time someone makes an excuse. Ask your colleagues if they have heard any good excuses lately. And, of course, take every opportunity to highlight the significant benefits of positive, proactive thinking and realizing that after all there is no such thing as a problem, since *every problem, and associated excuse, is really an opportunity waiting to be solved*. With the right mind-set, you, your colleagues, and your customers can solve each and every one in a positive, efficient, and mutually beneficial way. Excuse making no more!

"If you really want to do it, you do it. There are no excuses."
Bruce Nauman

Summary

1. Becoming aware of excuses and excuse making, both in you and in others, is the first concrete step toward eliminating them.
2. Be aware that every excuse comes with underlying reasons, or catalysts, for the excuse making in the first place. Professional salespeople know the significant benefits to be realized by unearthing these reasons and using them ethically to their benefit.
3. Excuse making, although deep-rooted, can be stopped and a newer, better approach of taking positive action developed with a little patience and effort on your part!

Remember Only This

"Stop making excuses!"

Author's note: If you are interested I would like to invite you to submit one to three of your best sales-related excuses at http://www.SalesLeadership.com/BestSalesExcuses. Once I sort and collate them, I will then send you an electronic copy of the completed *Book of Sales Excuses*. You can choose to have your name added as the "author of the excuse" (for fun) or to keep the input anonymous. It should make for some interesting and fun reading!

5

Busting Procrastination

"My advice is to never do tomorrow what you can do today.
Procrastination is the thief of time."
Charles Dickens

The writing of this chapter was tough. As I wrote the other chapters with excitement, there was something that convinced me to keep pushing this chapter off. I had lots of excuses, all good and logical ones of course, but nonetheless, it was the last and toughest chapter to write. Now there may have be some poetic justice in this, but the reality is it did not need to be the last one written. For some reason, even thinking about procrastination put me in a space of putting it off for another day. "My ideas will be better tomorrow," "The other chapters will provide a great background for this chapter," "It won't take long to write once I start," and the list went on. It got so bad that when all the other chapters were written, I was still trying to think of ways of not writing this one. After a while I recognized I had simply run out of excuses, or reasons, to get it wrong or not write it! But maybe if I just skipped the chapter altogether, the book would still be complete and nobody would ever notice that this twelve-chapter book was actually supposed to be a thirteen-chapter book!

And so it is with procrastination. There is always an excuse, always a reason, and always a problem that puts off the need to start an action, whatever the action might be. Of course these actions can range from small actions (file paperwork; complete the last three visit reports; update my contact database) all the way to really big actions (I need to start prospecting; I need to look for a new job; I need to resolve this strategic customer issue). Procrastination is an age-old characteristic that all human beings have exhibited at some point in their lives—and with most of us exhibiting throughout our entire lives. But why is this, and does it need to be this way?

What Exactly is Procrastination?

In its simplest form, procrastination is the action of delaying or postponing something. Now what's interesting is in understanding whether the delaying or postponing is a one-off decision that when made allows the original action now to be started. Or, does procrastination happen for a second, then a third time, and continue like this until the action is no longer valid, or until you accept that you are simply not going to start it. Based on this, there seems only to be a few possible outcomes of procrastination:

1. You procrastinate once, and then when the thought or requirement to start the action happens again, you do actually start the action.
2. You procrastinate once, then again, and then potentially multiple times, until the action becomes so critical that not completing it now would cause pain for you or others. You then start the action.
3. You procrastinate once, then again, and then potentially multiple times, until the action is no longer critical and decide it no longer needs to be completed (phew!).
4. You procrastinate once, twice, thrice, and in fact continue to procrastinate ad infinitum. The action never gets done, and the procrastination, excuse making, etc., continues indefinitely.

As you read through these four scenarios, I am sure your mind is bringing up thoughts of some procrastination you currently have: "I need to go to the gym," "I need to call the new procurement director," "I need to stop procrastinating." We all have our list, and few people actually reach the utopia state of not having any. The goal of the professional salesperson is to keep procrastinating to an absolute minimum, now and in the future, and always ensure that the big tasks, no matter how challenging or intimidating, are always tackled in a timely manner.

Why Do We Procrastinate?

In sales there are always a significant number of actions just waiting to be started. When busy handling lots of customer inquiries, opportunities and challenges, you will be in a constant state of busyness. When you have fewer customers, and less immediate work, professional salespeople will always ramp up their networking and prospecting activities to become busy with customers or soon-to-be customers. Quite simply there is always a lot to do, and therefore the existence of multiple and conflicting priorities—the trick is in identifying the important from the non-important, and the urgent from the non-urgent.

People procrastinate for lots of different reasons—including laziness, fear, embarrassment, perceived lack of skills, hope of the action naturally disappearing, in addition to a long list of others that are quite common and used by many. Some may even argue that procrastination was in fact the right decision, therefore justifying their inaction and actually further training themselves to procrastinate again in the future.

Moving the Big Rocks

I am sure everyone has heard the story of the classroom exercise where students have a range of materials to put into a glass container. The goal is to get all the materials into the container without anything being left over or overflowing. Many students will start off with the available sand since it makes a good base at the bottom of the container. Then they add the slightly larger gravel-like material. Once completed, they add the bigger stones, but quickly find they cannot get all the stones in the jar. This example is also close to the reality of managing procrastination. Many people keep themselves busy by doing the smaller actions first, and then don't have the time, energy, inclination, or courage to do the bigger, more important actions. This is often known in sales as "focusing on the busy work."

It is therefore important to start by putting in the big rocks and then adding the smaller gravel, then the sand, and finally filling up the jar with water! It will all fit into the jar, but only when things are added in the right order. So it is with sales—ALWAYS START WITH THE BIG ROCKS! Do the most important things first, then move to the smaller less important tasks, knowing that if your time or energy runs out, the key tasks are completed—the ones that will ultimately define and decide your sales success and career.

Repercussions of Procrastination

Wayne Gretzky, the great Canadian hockey legend, once remarked, "You miss one hundred percent of the shots you never take." Related to procrastination, this could mean waiting for a better opportunity (or the best opportunity), not embarrassing yourself with a miss (or multiple misses), or simply removing the pressure to make ANY shots! Gretzky was arguably the most prolific hockey player of all time, and indeed he missed many, many shots. But his scoring record was truly amazing and catapulted him into the Hockey Hall of Fame, becoming a genuine living sports legend!

There are always repercussions with procrastination. Some are immediate and known to you, while others take longer to materialize and not always directly known to you. No matter, everyone understands the simple concept of cause and effect, and the cause (procrastination) will indeed have a follow-on and likely negative outcome (effect) at some point in the future. This immutable fact cannot be disputed. So with this clear understanding, and realizing we cannot fight the laws of the universe, why do we consistently procrastinate, and why are we still procrastinating at this point in our life?

While working in Hong Kong a number of years ago, I managed a highly experienced sales director. He was a consistent and high performer, never prolific but always reliable. Something happened to him, and he began to procrastinate more frequently than normal, on lots of actions, both big and small. His free-flowing demeanor changed to be one of stress and excuse making, eventually causing him to leave the company to seek a new opportunity. Interestingly, and on reflection, nothing significant changed in his role except the requirement to make some necessary company-wide changes that were asked of all sales directors. He struggled with these seemingly easy changes, developed a strong reliance on procrastination, and soon built up a wall of actions and missed commitments that were simply impossible to recover from. But yet there was nothing that he could not do, if only he had put his mind to it and chosen to complete the actions successfully in the desired time. I often wonder if he is still choosing procrastination as his decision-making tool of choice—I hope not!

Can Procrastination Ever Be Positive?

I feel as though I am walking on quicksand even broaching this subject. However, it is a fair question. Can procrastination ever be positive, and more importantly is it a skill that can be developed and used effectively on occasion? The answer to the first part of the question is YES! I am sure everyone has heard of a story of someone procrastinating to do something and the subsequent outcome being inherently positive. There are numerous recollections from people on the never-to-be-forgotten day of 9/11. These people procrastinated for some reason or another and never made it to one of the collapsed buildings. Their lives were saved by simply not being there. Although this is a highly unusual example, no one can deny the true and amazingly heartfelt benefit of their stories—they are living proofs of it! So with this undeniable evidence, should we procrastinate more frequently and never try to overcome it?

I can only offer a personal viewpoint here and will leave it to the readers to draw their own personal conclusions. I believe wholeheartedly that in the mainstay, people's lives will be better, more joyous, and more successful when procrastination is reduced to an acceptable minimum. Specifically for professional salespeople, reducing or even eliminating procrastination will lead directly to more throughput, more sense of accomplishment, more career advancement, and more overall sales success!

Typical Sales Procrastinations

I always look forward to coaching my clients. Most are in sales, and some are business owners. On our biweekly coaching sessions, topics are discussed and occasionally homework is taken. At the next session I often start by asking, "How did you get on with completing your homework?" I can honestly say (and with a smile on my face), that this question generated much of the material for chapter four on "Extinguishing Excuses." I also smile because in my own sales career I have used many of these excuses myself! I realized that few excuses are ever truly original, although many people making them seem to think so. Ultimately as I work through these "excuses" with my clients, many of them sound valid, and some genuinely are. However, these excuses often have a root of procrastination in them. The excuses have somehow taken a higher priority, and the outcome being the homework is not completed. With a little focused coaching at this stage, we can normally iron out the procrastination wrinkles, but in some cases it can take many sessions!

Some of the most common procrastinations in sales, and ones that I may(!) have used in the past, include the following (see how many you have or are currently using):

1. I am not really sure how to tackle this action.
2. I've never done this before.
3. I am not sure how long this action will take.
4. I know the outcome will not be positive when this is done.
5. I won't be able to find all the resources I need.
6. It's probably more hassle than it's worth.

7. This will only lead to more actions.
8. I have other higher priority actions.
9. If I leave it, it might go away.
10. I need more information before I start.

As you will now likely realize, procrastination is the close partner of excuse making; they always seem to go hand in hand. The excuse in effect becomes both the excuse and the procrastination— powerful or what? Due to the potentially huge negative power and consequences of both excuses and procrastination, I decided to split them into two chapters, dealing with the challenges of each separately. They are worthy of a standalone chapter each since I have seen so much evidence of both being displayed in professional sales environments!

Procrastination Busting Mastery Tips

Most professional salespeople have more energy in the early part of their day compared to the latter, when things get busy and you are invariably doing a lot of running around. It's very interesting that as things get busier, if you recognize a task as being more challenging in some way, your natural reaction will be to put if off until a later time—procrastination in action! What is also clear is that if an action is considered easier, fun or simply one that you like doing, you will always seem to find the time for it, no matter what time of day it is, or your current level of energy. So unless you are one of those rare people that magically have more energy the further into the day you get, then it makes sense to get the big actions, especially the ones you have been procrastinating over, done as early in your day as possible.

When the big rocks are done in the early part of your day, you gain an immediate sense of accomplishment, and it will actually motivate you to get more done throughout the remainder of that day. Now, if the actions that are easy for you, or ones you particularly like, are now on your calendar, you will tackle them even more easily and with even more joy. In fact this staging of actions helps build momentum in your day, which leads to more energy, more belief in yourself and a more positive attitude. This directly and unequivocally leads to more sales success!

I once worked with a brilliant Director of sales. He had a large team, a large and growing sales budget and lots of actions, both internally and externally. He managed his time extremely well, and always managed to look and feel in control. I learned from him a little trick that can easily be applied to procrastination. He understood the psychology of procrastination well enough, and his own propensity to move to procrastination for big, or difficult, actions. He very intelligently added a section into his Day-Timer system. It was space to reflect each day on the things he was currently procrastinating on. It was a simple, but yet incredibly powerful system; since all it did was bring to his attention the actions he was currently putting off. This new awareness, and the fact he had to write it down daily at the start of his morning office routine, allowed him to take control of them, and get more of the big, important actions completed in a timely manner. He later told me it was always difficult for him, but the daily reminder was just the right amount of encouragement he needed. He subsequently developed his career so rapidly, that he is now the CEO of a major private company!

> *"Procrastination is the bad habit of putting of until the day after tomorrow what should have been done the day before yesterday."*
> **Napoleon Hill**

Summary

1. Procrastination is a normal, inherent condition in all humans but gets significantly stronger when it is allowed to develop unchecked.
2. Resolving procrastination requires both a system and a daily check-in, and the continuous use of patience to stop the triggers that start it in the first place.

3. You will immediately receive significant benefits, and in many forms, by tackling procrastination immediately.

Remember Only This

"Just do it now!"

THE
CREATING
HABIT

(Developing Lasting Traits)

6

Mastering Time

"Time stays long enough for those who use it."
Leonardo da Vinci

ime is just like the weather—most people feel they must make regular comments about it! Both seem to be universally discussed topics virtually every day by everyone on the planet. Both have a significant bearing on our lives but only one can be controlled! Understanding that time is something that is ultimately in your control, is the first step to realizing its power as a professional salesperson, and subsequently reaping the rewards of time mastery. The goal of this chapter is to enable you to become so proficient with the use of time, that you will surely become a master of it!

So What Exactly is Time?

A good starting point is to try and define, to really understand, what time is, and by doing so begin to realize what we are all dealing with. Time in the classical sense seems to be well understood by everyone: 60 seconds in a minute, 60 minutes in a hour, 24 hours in a day, 7 days in a week, etc. With a watch, a calendar or whatever means you use to track time, it is relatively straightforward to know exactly where you are in this linear measure. Today quickly becomes yesterday, tomorrow soon enters as today, and so the cycle continues, relentlessly! Just like gravity, time seems to affect us all in exactly the same way, yet there are marked differences in performance, and what professional salespeople can achieve in a given amount of time. But why? Sure, it could be related to available sales skills, to a person's inner drive, their experiences and indeed a whole lot more variables—but ultimately it's simply about what they choose to do with their available time.

You should understand clearly, choices about how you use your time are within your own control. Of course some companies and some roles in a professional sales environment, have predetermined time slots for certain things, whether it's to attend the next sales meeting on Tuesday at 9am, or attend customer meetings between Monday–Friday, 1:00–5:00p.m. But even within these and the other available time slots, there is a significant amount of control, which is your responsibility to use for maximum effect. How can you begin to think about time and through this begin to unlock its incredible power for you?

Measuring Your Time Usage

The old management saying, "You can only manage what you can measure" seems appropriate for helping unlock the power of time. Although most people have watches, or equivalents, to tell them what time of day it is, and choose to check it at multiple points throughout a typical day, most don't fully understand how they use their time. As a simple test, take a few minutes and note down how many hours (exactly) you worked per day for the last 20 working days. If you can do this with any degree of accuracy, you are automatically in the Top 1% of sales professionals who manage their time (and likely their performance)—congratulations! Now take the next part of the test and see if you can split this time usage into major categories. Choose your categories (between 6 and 10 are appropriate initially), and include ones that really align with how you spend your time. Examples to choose from may include:

1. E-mail management.
2. Travel time.

3. Sales/management/internal meetings.
4. Networking/prospecting.
5. Customer visits.
6. Proposal generation.
7. Customer research.
8. Thinking/creative time.
9. Break time (including breakfasts, lunches, coffees, etc.)
10. Miscellaneous (all the other time absorbing things that seem to happen in a typical day).

Understanding time usage at this second level of detail is critical to taking control of how you use your available time! Now let's get back to the total time you spend working per day. As I coach professional salespeople I invariably ask them the question "How many hours do you work per week?" Interestingly I have never had anyone phrase the answer in a way that says, "I work a maximum of . . ." Instead EVERYONE says, "I work a MINIMUM of . . ." The consistency of these answers gives an immediate clue to how people think about time, and especially time related to their work and careers.

For example, try this additional time test, and see how much you really know about your entire time usage and not just your work time. Split your life into six to eight categories (that will suffice for now). Examples could include:

1. Working time
2. Commuting time
3. Family time
4. Hobby time
5. "Me" time
6. Sleep time
7. Etc.

Start by taking (say) the last 7 days (include both work and non-work days), and detail how much time you allocated to each category. If you can do this test well and consistently, you are measuring your time exceptionally well—congratulations again! Now, whether you measure your time usage exactly or don't measure it at all, you will probably have some opinion as to how much time you want to spend on the various categories as your ideal template. An example might be for a typical week I want to spend 5 hours commuting to work, 45 hours working, 56 hours sleeping, 14 hours with the kids, 14 hours with my partner, 5 hours exercising, 14 hours relaxing, etc. Remember there are only 168 hours in a normal week! Now, if each of these categories is considered a time bucket, with each bucket containing the set number of hours noted above, the key questions to ask are:

1. Do I have the right number of time buckets to begin with?
2. Do I have a priority attached to each time bucket, knowing what ones are the most important?
3. Do I have the right number of hours in each of the time buckets to achieve life balance?
4. Do I have enough hours in my work time bucket to allow me to achieve all my sales goals?
5. Am I willing to have flexibility by using time from another bucket if I am short of hours in my working time bucket?
6. If I "borrow" time from one time bucket in a given week to use in another, do I replace that time in future weeks?

Re-addressing the Balance

Once you start measuring your time and comparing it against your ideal time allocation by category, consider using the "It's time to rebalance" test. The process works like this—note the periods you are using up more hours for your work time bucket, and note where you take the hours from (in my experience most people tend to take these hours from the family time bucket). If you have to work four more hours than your ideal this week and you take it from your family time, then commit to work four less hours at work next week, and replenish your family bucket, by allocating four more hours back to it. This might seem impossible, but I can say from firsthand experience it's certainly possible and, in fact, creates a system of flexibility for unexpected work challenges and opportunities that rebalances the family bucket by adding more time back to equalize it.

Interestingly when I ask professional salespeople what is more important—family or career—they will invariably say family, but yet this is the category (time bucket) that is normally the first to be drawn from when more work hours are required. This is a classic case of a misalignment in the "say-do gap"—saying one thing and doing another!

Finding and Increasing Smart Time

Once you begin analyzing how you allocate your work time, it should quickly be apparent that not all time should be considered equal when compared to results achieved. In fact with a little research, you will quickly see there is a distinct imbalance in *time input* compared to *results output*. This phenomenon has many names, including "The Pareto Principle," "The 80/20 Rule," and the "Law of the Vital Few." It is such a powerful and widespread phenomena that I have never seen it broken in business, or when applied to the time input and work output of a sales professional. The key principles of this rule related to sales performance are:

1. Eighty percent of revenues will come from twenty percent of your total work time.
2. Eighty percent of revenues will come from twenty percent of your total number of customers.

Note that the principle is highlighting the inequality of an input variable compared to an output variable, so it's not vitally important that eighty percent and twenty percent are the correct numbers for you—only that there is a significant imbalance in input and output that you must discover for your own sales business.

So if all this is true, and I now set you a goal of dramatically increasing your business, you may quickly spot that a smart way to do this is take the "magical twenty percent of your time" that is generating eighty percent of your revenues, and just double it. So you now use forty percent of your available time and in return get one hundred and sixty percent of your current performance. Assuming you are working five days per week, this equates to two days bringing in one hundred and sixty percent of your previous performance, and three days now bringing in fifteen percent of your previous performance—a net total of one hundred and seventy five percent. That's heading toward a doubling of your business with only a small change of focus! Logically this all makes sense, but somehow the vast majority of sales professionals don't think this way and so miss the opportunity of dramatically increasing their business. If we consider performance in this example to be revenues achieved, then I have heard many reasons from sales professionals for them not dramatically increasing performance:

1. You need the low-revenue customers to have the high-revenue customers.
2. The high-revenue customers come from working all the customers, and seeing which ones filter to the top.
3. Nobody can have an unfair proportion of high-revenue customers.
4. You need to keep working the low-revenue customers in case some of the high-revenue ones disappear.
5. Business is tough, so I cannot drop any of my low-revenue customers just in case.

It's clear that changing your percentages and thus increasing your revenues is really a strategy and a state of mind that you must employ. I have seen highly successful sales professionals earn significant sums of money by truly understanding the power of this law of imbalance and knowing how to instinctively apply it to their business. Whether you move toward doubling your business (or better), or whether you need a ten percent or twenty percent increase in your performance, thinking and implementing *The 80/20 Rule* is a smart choice. Gradually build this strategy up step-by-step into your weekly routine, and you will begin to transition your business to higher levels of revenue success. And lastly, if you get to two hundred percent revenue performance using this approach, implement it again and see if you can get to three hundred percent!

Time Mastery Best Practices

Once you have mastered the measuring, categorizing and balancing of your time, and have identified and implemented the key elements of *The 80/20 Rule* within your own sales practice, try these ten best practices to further boost your mastery of time and through these your sales results!

1. **Know your goals in as much detail as possible:** As you create your daily, weekly, monthly, quarterly and annual sales goals, do so by adding as much detail as possible. This will bring more clarity and focus to your day-to-day efforts, and benefit you by spending less time constantly thinking about strategy. Get your strategy (goals) right at the outset and then drive daily to make them happen.

2. **Find quiet time and a creative thinking space:** Insight comes from the times of silence that allow your mind to access universal knowledge. It is often called intuition, creativity or hunches. All come when you give yourself time and quiet. Try and find a creative place that provides a catalyst for this to happen.

3. **Understand that actions always incur time:** Develop an acute understanding that every action taken (or noted) is a future user of your time. Don't run with a calendar for appointment scheduling and a separate to-do list. Instead transpose all of your actions into your calendar with the correct priority and time allocated to each. A one-system approach is by far and away the most robust.

4. **Realize what is random and what is not:** Oftentimes the *miscellaneous* time bucket is the one that causes people the most challenge. The reason is they mistakenly believe most of what happens there is random is nature and difficult to predict. Become a student of this time bucket and you will surely realize that much of what happens is actually predictable in some manner.

5. **Build in "slack" time:** Once you start transposing actions into your calendar (since all actions take time), it is important and necessary not to load yourself above a certain level. My own system flags up when I am at 80 percent of my total time allocation. That alerts me to start scheduling non-urgent items into subsequent weeks, and keep as much of the remaining time for the important and miscellaneous actions that always seem to crop up at the last minute.

6. **Learn the discipline of time blocking:** Without doubt, time masters understand the power of time blocking in their week. For sales professionals this is especially important since there can be so many demands on your time, often with many of them conflicting. Normally, networking and prospecting activities are the first to fall of the priority list, yet they are a key determinant of future sales success. Time block accordingly and stick with your plan.

7. **Be ruthless with e-mail:** In today's e-mail intensive business environment, most professional salespeople will receive one hundred plus e-mails per day—even thinking about this is crazy! Learn to be ruthless with e-mail and strive to look at every e-mail only once. The simplest and most effective system I have seen is once an e-mail is read (or scan read if it's less important), action it immediately if it only takes a few minutes, delete it, file it, delegate it, or add it to your calendar as a future action with the right

priority and time attached to it. Then move swiftly to the next e-mail. Lastly, do e-mail once, or preferably, twice per day, but no more—we mistakenly believe that e-mail is the most urgent of all communication methods and tend to treat it in real time—don't!

8. **Develop the skill of knowing how long actions take to complete:** As you transpose actions into your calendar, develop the skill of becoming more accurate at forecasting how long an action will take to complete. The higher your accuracy, which naturally develops over time, the more control you will have of your calendar and the time you work.

9. **Learn to say no:** One of my favorite quotes is from Sir Richard Branson which states "Life is a lot more fun when you just say yes!" I resonate strongly with this quote but the beauty and subtlety of it lies in saying YES to the big and important things, and NO to the smaller and less important things. In sales, saying no is a developed skill and strength when used wisely, and on occasion.

10. **Start your day off consistently (the best possible way):** The truly successful sales professionals realize having a positive routine that is consistent and allows them to start their day off well, is key to daily and long-term success. Whether it's exercising to boost your energy and get you focused, or taking some quiet time for meditation, to spending some quality time with your kids, choose something that inspires you and fuels you for the normal and expected challenges and opportunities that you will undoubtedly face.

As a closing comment, time mastery does take time! If you can faithfully implement the ideas contained within this chapter you elevate yourself to such a small minority of all sales professionals, you will be truly amazed. Interestingly it's this small minority that is easily identified as the most prolific and successful of all sales professionals— the Top1%! Coincidence or not?

"Until you value yourself, you wont value your time. Until you value your time, you will not do anything with it."
M. Scott Peck

Summary

1. Learn the skills, and develop the disciplines, of measuring and categorizing your time, and how to balance your various time buckets.
2. Use *The 80/20 Rule* to concentrate on smart time, which always turns out to be the most impactful, positive, and results-generating time.
3. Become an unceasing student of time mastery, and incorporate the tips and tricks of the time masters, the highest performers of the sales world.

Remember Only This

"Mastering time is the foundation of all success!"

7

Creating Momentum

"The world is wide, and I will not waste my life in friction,
when it could be turned into momentum."
Frances E. Willard

There is an old saying that "Success breeds success!" You may also have heard the expression that "Money begets money." Both these pieces of age-old wisdom have their basis in *momentum*. You can see it in almost every walk of life. On the sports field when a team is on a winning streak and appear unstoppable, to the professional salesperson who wins opportunity after opportunity, seemingly "doing everything right and being lucky!" There are also many similar examples of this concept related to individuals, teams, companies, organizations, and countries who believe in themselves enough to keep doing the right things consistently, one by one.

My favorite analogy I have used many times now to explain momentum, is the concept of the steam engine. When you see the coal man shovel the first pieces of coal into the small engine fire nothing apparently happens apart from the slowly increasing fire, some occasional puffs of steam and an occasionally hiss of noise. As the coal man continues to shovel load after load of coal into the engine, the fire gets brighter, the steam more plentiful and the noise louder. By consistently applying this approach of "feeding the fire" eventually the wheels of the train begin to turn ever so slowly, inch by inch. Somehow the train is being coaxed into movement. The coal continues to be added, and the whole process continues. Eventually, through this application of *doing the right things at the right time*, momentum is kick-started; the train builds up speed, steam billows from the funnel, with the commensurate noise that highlights rapid movement. Eventually the train reaches full speed—momentum now fully evident, and the coal man only needs to add an occasional load of coal to keep the train running at this speed. Interestingly, the coal man usually doubles as the train driver, and at this time he exudes an air of confidence and being in total control, having time to enjoy the scenery, have a cup of tea, and enjoy the great speed both he and the train are now witnessing. Voila—and so it is with momentum!

So What Exactly is Momentum?

Momentum is the outcome of applied force that creates positive movement. This force, related to a professional salesperson, is the set of consistent actions undertaken day-in and day-out, that creates positive movement toward his goals. It is the feeling that is created when you start to see signs you are heading in the right direction. It's something that is intuitive and comes from the inside—you just know that the actions you are doing are the right ones and will generate the success you are striving for. As you begin to see the early signs of success, this in itself builds more confidence, more passion and more energy to keep going. These elements allow you to tackle more, and tougher actions, thus creating even more momentum. At some point this consistency will allow you to hit a steady state of results, which align perfectly with your goals. If you are like me, at this stage you will likely look back and think, "How did I get here?" Quite simply you worked to "get here" and you deserve all the successes that naturally accompany this stage.

It's worthwhile to compare the building blocks of momentum for a professional salesperson and the coal man/train driver story above, to learn possible correlations:

1. There has to be a clear goal, or set of goals, at the outset that will harness the motivation to take action.

2. Action needs to start once the goal is clear—without focused action, movement toward your goal will be erratic at best.

3. It would appear easy to stop action once started, since impatience or other factors could easily creep in, and suggest the necessary results are not materializing quickly enough. Resist the urge to quit or change approach, and instead stay focused and keep doing the *right things at the right time*.

4. Results start materializing and your goals start being achieved. At this stage it would be wise to uncover what actions are required to keep momentum going at the pace you desire.

5. As you reach the state of hitting your goals consistently, be humble and thankful for your achievements. This will help keep your eye on the subsequent actions required, and stop possible complacency.

A few years ago when I was working for a multinational, high-growth company, I was tasked with taking a low-performing region (in fact the lowest performing of the 14 regions worldwide), and "turning it around." The five steps above were exactly the ones I used. I remember clearly the thoughts and emotions I encountered at each of the five stages:

1. **I wanted** to be seen as a sales professional capable of turning a region around and hitting its necessary goals. This created motivation within me.

2. I developed a strategy and subsequent action plan that **I believed** would be good enough to solve the challenges and achieve the region's goals.

3. I had to, on a number of occasions, re-convince myself that I was doing the right thing, and often had to hold back senior management from forcing another course of action, since **I felt** both my team and I were doing the right things.

4. **I hoped** that the results would continue, and invested time on a regular basis to check in against both the strategy and action plan, ensuring that results toward the goals continued.

5. **I accepted** the accolades from my team and senior management to the revenue recovery that had been created, but **I resisted** the temptation to become arrogant, complacent or self-inflated. This allowed the clarity necessary to stay focused, and thus achieve even higher performance over time.

How Do You Create Momentum?

When thinking about creating momentum you first have to realize that in most cases (just like the steam engine) you will be starting off from a baseline of zero on your imaginary scale. The purpose of gaining momentum is to accelerate toward the completion of your goals in the least amount of time and with the least amount of effort. Momentum creates positive movement and a commensurate belief that you are on the right track and doing the right things. It should be noted, however, that as momentum is gained it does not mean that things will get tougher or slower, or in any way more comfortable or uncomfortable for you. In my opinion, momentum should be considered to be a positive force in your life in the attainment of your goals, and not something that will make your life more difficult!

Consider a driver stepping into a car for the start of a journey. Initially the car is stationery, and so the driver starts the engine, and moves into first gear. As the car gains speed, second gear is now chosen, and then third, until the highest gear is being used. Momentum has been created, and high speed is now being achieved. Now, look at the driver—his actions are not so much different (if any) than when he was moving along in first gear—the same block-and-tackling actions, the same approach. If anything, he now has to be a bit more observant since things are happening much faster than before. However, the same basic principles and actions apply at low speed or high speed. It's exactly the same with the engine—the gears are changed to maximize both power and efficiency. The engine is basically doing the same thing whether in first gear or top gear. People mistakenly think that everything will change when they are in top gear, when they have full momentum. Of course some things will change, but the basics can never be discarded even at this point. Keep doing *the right things at the right time*, and you will create and subsequently maintain momentum.

Now try this simplified approach to creating momentum and helping achieve your sales goals:

1. **Develop a clear understanding of the goal(s) and outcome(s) you are seeking:** Be as specific as possible here with the details and choose to write them down. Oftentimes it's the writing of them that makes them more concrete and real for people, and of course allows them to be communicated and tracked much more readily.

2. **Determine opportunities for leverage:** Before you launch into the actions, take a moment and see if there are any leverage opportunities available. This is a key step and helps differentiate the highest performing sales professionals from the rest. This may include leveraging additional people, finances, systems, and processes. Don't move on to step 3 without having a clear understanding on how help can be attained. Remember this can be the determining stage for whether momentum will be created quickly or not.

3. **Implement the actions one by one:** Look for successes at each action completion. Use these completions (mini-outcomes) to boost your confidence that you are on the right track.

4. **Practice patience:** Know you will undoubtedly come across some actions that appear tougher to close successfully—if you still believe they are the right ones, stick with them and don't give up. Patience is certainly required here. This is also known as the testing phase in sales, and everyone has to go through it!

5. **Check in against your goals and outcomes to date:** This will ensure you are on track. Take some quality time to periodically review your strategy and test if it is still what it needs to be. Don't be afraid to make small tweaks and changes at this time—it's good practice to test the future applicability of your strategy based on the momentum you have achieved to date.

6. **Challenge yourself on acceleration ideas at this stage:** See if you can come up with more, smarter ways of accelerating progress toward your goals—remember think leverage and be clear in your understanding that success attracts success, so new leverage opportunities will likely reveal themselves to you, if you keep looking out for them.

7. **Be comfortable during the flow of momentum:** It's a different feeling than when you started, when you had to dig deep for self-motivation. Now the results are happening and you are attaining the expected outcomes to the goals you set. Be thankful for the success and continue to think and act positively by doing *the right things at the right time*. Resist the urge to be complacent now. The difference between success and massive success can often be a small difference of focused and sustained effort. Stick with it!

The Momentum Master Key—Leverage!

Defined simply, leverage is the power to influence a person or situation to achieve a desired outcome or goal. Leverage is the master key to achieving momentum in a manner that is consistent, smart and rapid. It involves an understanding of the dynamics of life, human beings and business that allow for an *acceleration of change*. Leverage implies using the natural immutable laws of the universe to your benefit.

Types of Leverage

Many people seem to create fantastic results and outcomes from the misuse, or even abuse, of people, money and systems. Stories abound where an individual or group have used such elements in a manner that is neither ethical nor moral. This type of leverage simply can never be accepted. Leverage therefore must take the higher ground and in so doing add benefit to everyone and everything at every available opportunity. Only through this type of ethical leverage can true success be attained.

In sales there always seems to be challenges encountered that test our ability to make ethical and moral decisions that are good for all concerned parties. These challenges must always be handled with an understanding that bringing benefits to you can and should involve bringing benefits to the other people also. This mentality comes from an understanding and belief in the age-old concept of abundance rather than scarcity.

A great example of this was the late well-known Scot, Andrew Carnegie, who was the father of the U.S. steel industry. He created massive leverage and through this made his 21-person mastermind team all multimillionaires. I suspect he could have withheld some of the financial benefits to these people, and come from a place of scarcity rather than abundance, if he so chose. His approach, however, is a perfect example of using leverage to create momentum, and through this enable the success of the people who helped create it in the first place. Of course one of the well-documented outcomes of this "mastermind group" strategy was that Andrew Carnegie became the richest man in the world, at that time!

Putting the Brakes on Momentum

When creating momentum, just as the quote at the beginning of the chapter suggests, friction is the enemy. But it's more than just friction, and in fact there are many factors that can stop momentum from taking place, or slow it down once started. Let's examine a few of the more common ones:

1. Not having a clear, consistent vision or strategy that stands the test of time.
2. Not having the courage to start something because of an excuse, or excuses, that you think cannot be overcome.
3. Not having the patience to stick with both strategy and actions to break through the barriers to success.
4. Becoming arrogant and taking your eye off the ball as you begin to see some early signs of success.
5. Abandoning what has worked successfully for you in the past by chasing something that you think is a lot easier (the principle of getting something for nothing).

In my many years in sales I have never quite seen momentum happening at exactly the rate that someone wanted it to. Oftentimes it's faster than expected and even more frequently it's slower. But it should be noted that the rate of momentum can change over the course of attaining your goals—things can speed up and things can slow down. Be alert to clues and determine if changes are required to speed up, or if the application of a little patience is merely what's required.

Ten Ideas for Creating Sales Momentum

It's clear that the most accomplished sales professionals exhibit a set of approaches and methods to their role that brings them consistent success. Of course even the best sales professionals will have times of challenge, but at this juncture they continue to do *the right things at the right time* based on their knowledge and experience. One of the best-known business personalities who is also a consummate salesperson is Donald Trump. He is well known for his outgoing, opinionated approach to life. However, many people may not know he was actually a billionaire before becoming bankrupt. By using the skills previously learned, he created the business and sales momentum he once had, and thus *regained* his billionaire status. The right actions, implemented at the right time consistently, will always pull you through to the success you plan for and desire.

Try these ten ideas for creating momentum, and then see if you can add another ten specific to your own circumstances:

1. Time block—it helps with consistency in applying actions.
2. Recount and promote successes—they are fuel for the *Law of Attraction*.
3. Laugh at apparent failures—spend less time thinking about them and more on positive action.
4. Seek out people who are momentum and success conscious—they are contagious.
5. Choose to do something every day toward your goals, no matter how small the action.
6. For every strategy and action think about the potential of leverage in some way.
7. Don't deviate from your strategy.
8. Keep your eyes open for synchronicities (these are coincidences you decide to take action on).
9. Create light processes as you go along—make them simple, highly repeatable and easy to implement.
10. Simply believe that you can do it—employ daily positive affirmations—they do work if you try them!

"Success requires first expending ten units of effort to produce one unit of results. Your momentum will then produce ten units of results with each unit of effort."
Charles J. Givens

Summary

1. Everyone creates momentum to some degree or other; raise your own bar and use the concept of momentum to achieve

more goals, with more sustainable results, and faster than ever before.

2. Understanding the concept of leverage and applying it to every opportunity, provides for massive acceleration towards the achievement of your goals through increased momentum.

3. Know that creating and maintaining momentum is a process that can and should be learned early, and applied as often as possible.

Remember Only This

"Leverage creates momentum to achieve
your goals faster!"

8

Manifesting Synchronicities

"Synchronicity is an ever present reality for those who have eyes to see it."
Carl Jung

When I decided to write this book, I chose key topics that I felt were appropriate for sales professionals based on my own experiences in sales and sales leadership. In fact after I had completed the book, all ready to send to the printers, I decided something was missing. I knew instinctively it was a chapter on synchronicity and its amazing power when used consistently, but I also knew it was a difficult subject to explain well, even although we have all experienced it on many occasions in our business and personal lives. So, I reluctantly (but happily) made the decision to include a chapter on it, albeit a shorter chapter than the others. It really is a fascinating subject and one I am only in the early stages of understanding myself, but I believe that sales professionals who are ultra-successful, the Top 1%, either consciously or subconsciously manifest these synchronicities in their lives. But the question is how?

What Exactly is Synchronicity?

The first challenge is to define synchronicity since many people will have heard about it but may not be able to explain it. Synchronicity is a phenomenon that arises where something of coincidence becomes known through forces no one fully comprehends, and because of this you decide to take positive, affirmative action on the coincidence. It's really that simple!

A synchronicity and a coincidence are very close cousins but different. A coincidence can be considered as a random event that happens in which you choose not to take any positive action. A synchronicity is the same as a coincidence except now you choose to take positive action. I am sure you have said and heard many people say, "That was a coincidence." What it basically means is that something, apparently random in nature, has occurred that is *interesting* in some way, enough to make you think for even a split second. It could be a chance meeting, an unexpected e-mail, or anything that in some way has come into your life that gets you to think about it in some curious way.

The reality is that when alerted by a coincidence, most people choose to do nothing about it. If anything, it becomes merely interesting, but insignificant, a random event in our lives. If the event has caused more than a split second of thought, we may choose to mention it to someone else. Some examples are "I bumped into John today at the coffee shop," "I was thinking about a new job, and I received an e-mail from a headhunter," and "I was surfing the web and found a really great holiday destination and could really use a vacation right now." Without action they are merely conversation topics with friends. And of course with coincidences, as soon as they enter your mind and quickly processed, they will more likely than not leave just as fast, never to return. The synchronicity opportunity now gone!

How Do You Manifest Synchronicities?

I can share my own experiences of how to manifest synchronicities, although I suspect I am only scratching the surface of the real potential that could be achieved. I have been through periods of massive synchronicities manifesting themselves, multiple times a day, and then times when apparently nothing seems to be happening. Drawing some conclusions, it is apparent that my state of mind was front and center to this phenomenon. When I was thinking (and acting) in a highly positive manner with great belief that I could achieve anything I wanted, coincidences happened more frequently. What was also extremely interesting was knowing my state of mind was so positive, I was much more inclined to seriously think about the coincidences and then act on them, to create something positive in my life. The more I seemed to do this, the more coincidences would appear.

Now at this stage you are probably asking if synchronicities are still happening at a rapid rate for me, and if not, why not? What I have noticed is that coincidences seem to come in waves when they are acted on as synchronicities, then seem to dry up. I believe that if you were to do some controlled research on this, you would find a direct correlation between positive thinking and the amount of synchronicities that manifest. Life always seems to have a way of challenging everyone when they are in full flow by "testing their mettle" to stay positive no matter what. The reality is there are only a few individuals who somehow manage to stay super-positive in almost (and apparently) all situations, no matter what life throws at them. For the rest of us, we naturally and regularly experience the ups and downs in our moods, positivity, and beliefs depending on our own particular set of life circumstances. I have noticed coincidences coming and going in my life—sometimes more, sometimes less, sometimes being acted upon to become synchronicities, and sometimes staying merely as coincidences.

I have also noticed when I go through a normal cycle of "feeling okay about life" and NOT feeling amazing, coincidences are few and far between. However, when I wake up in the morning and think I can conquer the world and do anything that I put my mind to, coincidences begin to re-appear again after a period of consistent positive thinking. It may be days, weeks, or even months, but with patience there is no doubt they start up again. I then go through the cycle of transforming my coincidences into synchronicities by taking affirmative and positive action. At these special times in my life, I have felt the most alive, the most positive, and the most connected to a source far greater than myself. It also feels like I am driving at maximum speed in top gear, and my life in some shape or form is taking a big leap forward—and it normally does!

You will undoubtedly have experienced this yourself, when everything seems to be going right for you, when "the wind is at your back" experiencing the amazing joys of life. Quite simply, at this stage, life can only be described as great! Then something will begin to test you in ways that are highly specific and personal to you. Maybe a deal will not close as you had forecast it would, or you start getting a bit complacent, thinking that everything you are involved in will automatically materialize. Whatever it is, know that something will happen to test you. You then need to consciously decide what your mental attitude will be at that point and what action, if any, you will now choose to take. Many people, and in my opinion most people, will now put the brakes on their accelerated progress in some way. It could be feeling sorry for themselves, allowing procrastination to creep back again, choosing not to take positive action when another coincidence happens, or simply allowing negative thinking to enter their minds again and take root. When any of these things happen, know that coincidences and subsequently synchronicities will begin to quickly dry up!

How Many Synchronicities Can I Manifest?

I have never counted the amount of coincidences I have manifested into synchronicities through positive action, but I know it has been quite a few. As to how many can a person manifest, I believe the number is in fact infinite and is more controlled by our state of mind (positivity and self-belief), and our corresponding desire to take action. We have all encountered people who seem to have a great run, where everything seems to be going right for them, where opportunities seem to happen almost automatically, and they somehow manage to fully realize these opportunities. In most cases it looks like they are doing all of this quite unconsciously, in a state requiring little effort. Of course, there is effort, even if we are not fully aware of it.

I believe, therefore, it's UNIMPORTANT to actually count synchronicities since they only manifest when coincidences happen, and you subsequently initiate the right, positive action. Without doubt an element of trust is also required. Choose to trust in the universe, and you will be given the opportunity of having access to as many coincidences and synchronicities as you can handle. The universe seems to be very smart that way and consistently resists giving things to people who don't use them wisely!

What Stops Synchronicities from Happening?

Synchronicities appear to be cyclical, but that is only my own experience. I actually suspect they are as plentiful as the air we breathe, if only we could learn to breathe properly! It's clear, however, that embarking on certain things will stop synchronicities, and sometimes so rapidly it will have you wondering what just happened. Consider the following list to see if they resonate with you, then try to add a few from your own experiences:

1. Thinking negatively.
2. Counting synchronicities.
3. Choosing not to share benefits.
4. Choosing not to act on a coincidence.
5. Trying to force synchronicities to materialize.
6. Thinking of scarcity.
7. Not following your personal vision and goals.

What is interesting is that even if you don't believe in synchronicities, the universe will still try and get you interested in them by providing coincidences in your life. After thinking about a coincidence, be bold and follow your gut feel by taking affirmative and positive action. Voila—another synchronicity in action!

Should Every Coincidence Be Acted Upon?

This is an interesting question, and one I quite simply don't know the answer to. My experiences, however, lead me to believe that a more appropriate question is, "When a coincidence happens and I really think about it and identify a meaningful action, do I then choose to implement the action?" I have experienced on quite a few occasions a coincidence happening in my life, subsequently thinking about it, but then not being able to identify a meaningful action, and thus letting go of the opportunity to manifest it into a synchronicity. Instead of believing that every coincidence should be acted upon, think that each should be fully considered to determine if an action is evident. Finding meaningful and positive actions is a skill that needs to be developed over time and requires both trust and creativity in equal measures.

Steps to Manifest Synchronicities

It seems that manifesting synchronicities requires simply doing the opposite of what naturally stops synchronicities. Maybe this is obvious, but what intrigues me here is that there does not appear to be a gray area, a middle zone. Synchronicities like a binary approach, so, for example, being slightly positive is not enough—that's sitting in the gray zone! Instead, choosing total positivity as your thinking approach will surely get things kick-started. In my experience, most people like to play it safe by doing things to a certain degree, but not fully committing themselves. Choose to commit yourself fully to the right things and watch those synchronicities stack up one by one!

Consider these eight points that I know have some degree of influence on making coincidences happen, and subsequently synchronicities to manifest:

1. **Think positively:** By consistently and genuinely thinking positively, you will build up your confidence, which will

shine through to everyone around you. Positive thinking is contagious and seems to be the single biggest activator of coincidences.

2. **Believe in the abundance model:** It's clear the world is rich with possibilities. Having a fundamental belief that life is not meant to be tough or cause continuous hardship, and instead believing there is abundance all around and in all aspects of life, will activate the *Law of Attraction* and hence synchronicities.

3. **Stay positive:** Slightly different from point 1, this refers directly to your reactions when something challenging happens in your life. Challenging things happen to everyone at various points, so choose not to take them personally and do not allow them to stop the positive flow in your life. These challenges will likely test you, but that might just be their purpose in the first place!

4. **Be continually thankful:** There is a great positive power attached to being genuinely thankful for life's blessings. When good things happen, and especially when they come thick and fast, remember to take the time and be thankful for them in a way that is both meaningful and personal to you. Don't fake this important task, and only you will know whether you do or not.

5. **Don't get cocky or arrogant:** Likely you have seen this occur in other people, where things are going extremely well and they are receiving many positive benefits. Then apparently "out of the blue," they become arrogant and too full of their own importance. When this happens, not only do I believe synchronicities begin to dry up for them, but I also believe they put themselves on the slippery slope of life, which will surely over time help them realize the error of their thinking.

6. **They appear cyclical—don't get discouraged:** It appears that just like waiting for a bus and none arriving, if you wait a bit longer, a few will arrive at the same time! Coincidences seem to appear in cycles and in batches, and these phases have unknown durations. They will more than likely dry up, but consider this only to be a test that will genuinely challenge your resolve. Keep doing the right things at this stage, and the coincidences and subsequent synchronicities will kick-start themselves when the time is right.

7. **Follow your life's true purpose:** When you become completely clear what you want to do and be in life, and align your decisions and actions accordingly, bolstering this with an incredibly positive attitude and faith that it will happen, then synchronicities will start appearing very quickly for you—hold on tight!

8. **Take action:** After our discussion in this chapter, it would appear that this is both obvious and necessary, but often (quite often!) most people choose not to take any type of action. The coincidence sets-up the opportunity of the synchronicity manifesting, and all you have to do to make it real is to take meaningful and positive action. Easy or what?

So, I did say it was a short chapter, but hopefully one that really made you think and reflect on situations, events, and outcomes in your own life. Coincidences will always happen to you at a rate that is somehow linked to your positivity and self-belief that they will happen. Taking quality time to think if there is an affirmative and positive action available, and then making the action happen, will allow you to manifest the synchronicity and the significant benefits coming from it. And it will allow more synchronicities to happen again in the future!

"There is no such thing as chance; and what seem to us merest accident springs from the deepest source of destiny."
Friedrich Schiller

Summary

1. Coincidences happen to everyone. Choosing to positively act on them can create synchronicities and through this highly beneficial outcomes.
2. Synchronicities appear to happen in waves. Have your surfboard ready and waiting!
3. Manifesting further synchronicities in your life requires trust in the universe and an undying positive attitude under all circumstances.

Remember Only This

"Think and act on a coincidence, then watch the synchronicity manifest itself!"

THE OFFERING HABIT

(Creating Mutually-Aligned Benefits)

9

Selling Values

*"Real integrity is doing the right thing, knowing that nobody's
going to know whether you did it or not."*
Oprah Winfrey

Every day in sales we come across companies who have mission statements, vision statements and a corresponding set of guiding values that help them attract and retain employees, and supply guidelines to them on how they should grow the business over time. These elements seem necessary to starting a company and helping transform it into a success. We will concentrate this chapter on the vital area of *values*—and include both personal and company values.

I recall an old sales story you may have heard already. It captures the actions of a seasoned salesperson who loved Italian shoes. He would wear them at every internal and external meeting, and in fact had numerous pairs to choose from. One day the Chief Financial Officer of the company noticed the salesperson was claiming these shoes on his expenses. The CFO immediately complained strongly to the Vice President of sales and said the company would no longer support this type of expense, and in fact he was never made aware that the salesperson in question was claiming for shoes. He immediately asked the VP of sales to find out why the salesperson was claiming the shoes in the first place. After a little research the VP came back and told the CFO the Italian shoes made the salesperson feel more confident and with this added confidence he was better able to represent the company, and hence win more deals! The CFO was dismayed by this response and received immediate assurances from the VP that the salesperson would no longer claim for his shoes. A few months then passed, when the CFO commented to the VP he had been checking the salesperson's expenses in detail, and was happy to report that he was no longer claiming for his expensive Italian shoes. The VP retorted, "You don't think so?"

In this simple, but likely true scenario, transparency was the value, and the salesperson chose not to live it by hiding future shoe expenses amongst other expenses. In this case he managed to get away with it (at least so far), even under the close scrutiny of the CFO. In today's ultra-transparent world, the only way of operating both within your company and with customers is with complete transparency and impeccable values!

How Can We Define Values?

Of course there are many definitions of values, what they mean, and what they should be used for. My own personal definition is the set of guides that are intrinsic to me as a human being, that stay with me at all times, always letting me know "the right thing to do." They are guides because ultimately I always have free choice to decide what I will do in any given situation. However, my own personal values are deeply entrenched, so much so that I don't need to think about them—they are automatic in response, and highlight the way I choose to lead every aspect of my life. Now, can I say that in every situation in my life I have stuck 100 percent to my values—no! As I get older though, and maybe a little wiser, I realize even more the power of values and being completely and utterly consistent in their application. And so to it is with all sales professionals—you have to decide what your own set of values are, how consistently you want to use them, and in what situations.

Another definition that may resonate with you is the old adage of "treating people the way you would want to be treated". In other words the thoughts and actions that are applied by other people toward you! Values develop over time and can change, but your primary set of values will be quite well developed by now and unlikely to change significantly moving forward. They reside within your personal DNA, and have been influenced by your parents, teachers, religious leaders and your own personal environment—a lot of input in which to form these lifelong guides!

It's interesting to note that both individuals and companies have values. What's even more interesting is that companies have a great need to create, publish and continually communicate their values to their employees, but as individuals we don't! In fact we often tend to keep our personal values quite close, and it's only people that know us quite well (family, friends, close colleagues) that get to understand our values to some degree or another, and this happens mostly through seeing us in action, and then interpreting what our values are. If values are so important in life, why do we tend to hide them so well to the majority of people? A professional salesperson can, and should, therefore choose to more openly communicate as well as seek out personal values. Let's investigate further . . .

Why Should We Care About Values?

It's clear when dealing with individuals at a company, we are unlikely to know at an early stage what is truly important to them, both from a company standpoint and from an individual standpoint. Part of the selling cycle must be to discover as much about their company and personal values as possible, and in the least amount of time. Company values are often disclosed on their website, normally in the ABOUT US section, but also in the HIRING section. If they are not included there, simply look around within their office when you are next there, since company values are inevitably displayed on walls, especially in meeting and conference rooms. If all else fails, simply ask your contact at the company, and they will likely share them with you happily.

Knowing these company values is exceptionally important in dealing with the customer. This is their own set of governing principles that supply guidance to how they encourage employees to think and act, both internally and externally. And that also means in dealing with people just like you! Get to know a company's value set before you make a call to them or step inside their offices. It can make a huge difference later on and will only strengthen your knowledge of the customer, what they are about, and help create the right strategy to work with them successfully. It should be abundantly clear that any sales professional who blatantly exhibits traits and actions that are different from a customer's core values will likely struggle to get business—it really is that simple. So be prepared and take a little time to do your homework.

One of my executive coaching clients works for a great company who believe that going above and beyond the call of duty, if there is a big customer issue, is so important and fundamental to them, they included it in their list of top ten company values. To be more explicit, they chose to include in the list an event that once happened unexpectedly in the past. The value statement reads, "We will do everything possible to help a customer in need, including hiring out a helicopter!" The story refers to a customer who urgently needed a replacement part, and the only viable way to get it to them quickly was hiring a helicopter. They did, managed the customer situation successfully, and created a unique value that is now clear to all employees and part of their company folklore. Simply brilliant!

Now, let's move on to the more complex subject of personal values within customers. As I coach people, especially at the senior level, I hear many of them talking about customers as "things" or "entities," but not as people! I believe that all companies, although they have their own dynamics, products, services, intellectual property, etc., are at their very core a collection of individuals, a collection of people. And we know that when dealing with people, it is important to have a basic connection and alignment with them if we are to successfully sell to them. This means taking the time to discover as much as we can about them and their personal and company values.

Know for sure, that if the customer senses any misalignment in their personal values and yours, then you will struggle, and may in fact never make a sale in the first place. So, is there in fact a risk in trying to discover the other person's values and seeking for common alignment, since potentially none may actually exist? Maybe, but in my own experience most people are open to sharing aspects about themselves, and once you get to know them a bit better, the majority will share some of their values with you. Other values that are not explicitly shared can often be interpreted through their expressions, words and actions. Again it's like playing a detective and digging around to uncover the things that are most important to them.

Should Values Be Part of the Selling Cycle?

Over the years I have found myself in some interesting conversations related to this question, "Should we consider values as part of the sales process, and if so, why?" My response has always been consistent, in that I don't think any professional salesperson actually has a choice. There are a variety of reasons for this:

1. Slowly but surely we are moving toward a values-based culture. It is a slow movement but there are numerous examples including furniture companies who only buy from sources of sustainable wood suppliers, to companies that add the value of fun into their guiding principles.
2. More people are beginning to ask themselves what their own values are, why they have them, and in so doing are being alerted to look for and align with other like-minded (values-minded) people.
3. Values ultimately reveal themselves in business, especially when a challenge is encountered. Many companies realize that a long-term business relationship will likely hits bumps along the way—and so they are seeking knowledge of what your, and your company's, values are at the outset.
4. In the natural course of communication and conversation, everyone gives clues to their own values. When you tune into this you can learn much about a person.

5. Alignment of personal values between you and your customer can be a significant competitive advantage if used appropriately.

It's clear that both personal and company values are here to stay. So don't shy away from discovering them, talking about them, or even on occasion debating them. When you truly become interested in people, you automatically become interested in their values. When that happens you will become much more natural at making a lasting connection with them. These lasting connections are a great way in helping to develop a mutually acceptable, long-term business relationship—and through this incremental SALES!

Matching Personal and Company Values

We have touched on the fact that most companies have a set of values often called guiding principles. What's noticeable is that not everyone who works for a company will share and exhibit exactly the same set of personal values, and interestingly both company and personal values may not be perfectly aligned. This is not so much the challenge of the professional salesperson, but more with the customer and their employees. However, companies generally do a great job of aligning the right people with their company's values, and so it is a fair assumption to expect the customer's representatives to exhibit them. On the rare occasion you notice something amiss, just be aware of it and any likely ramifications, and do your best to accept and work around it, while at the same time ensuring you are not in any way compromising your own values!

Values You Must Always Have

Values ultimately are a personal choice, and you can choose to have whatever ones you want, and use them in whatever circumstances you want. Over the years I have seen a minority of salespeople try and game the system, to gain an edge somehow by unethical means, or to simply mislead a customer in the hope of earning some advantage for themselves (normally a higher commission or bonus check). I can honestly say that none of them have been successful in the long term. Something always comes back to bite them along the way since they chose not to have, or apply consistent, long-term values. In today's hyper-transparent business environment, I believe there are certain values that simply must be in place to be successful, and to develop and maintain a long-term successful sales career. Here are my top ten recommendations (strong recommendations!) for all sales professionals:

1. Never, ever compromise on integrity.
2. Exhibit transparency in all your business interactions.
3. Chose to care about your customers and their success.
4. Communicate in a timely manner.
5. Treat all people with dignity and respect.
6. Listen, listen, and listen again.
7. Choose to see the best in people.
8. Believe in the concept of abundance, not scarcity.
9. Develop and practice perseverance and tenacity.
10. Do what you *instinctively* know is right.

I often share this values-related story, which I fondly call "my worst customer meeting!" I was working for a large multinational company in Scotland, and was only a few years into my budding career. The outcome of this story was not ideal, but it taught me a great deal about relationships, about values and about treating people with dignity and respect. I travelled four hours by car to meet with the customer. It was a long, hard drive with low clouds and driving rain. I was excited about meeting the Vice President of engineering, and the opportunity was a significant one, potentially millions of dollars of revenue for my company. I met the receptionist and was courteously shown to a modern, bright conference room upstairs. I waited patiently for my contact to arrive. I waited and waited. Eventually about 20mins after the scheduled start time for the meeting, he arrived. We had never met before since I had been dealing with members of his staff up to that point. He stood in the doorway and said the following:

"I won't introduce myself since you know who I am. We all know the reason you are here. I know the technical features of the device you are selling, so you don't need to tell me any of that. There is only one thing that I want to know from you. Can you sell me this device for $2.32 per unit for 1 million units? I know that this is a very low price and you likely don't have the seniority to authorize it. There's a phone in the middle of the conference room table, so I suggest you make a call to the people who can make a decision. Also I am a very busy guy, and my office is over there {pointing to a big corner office far from the conference room}. If you manage to get the price I need pop into my office and let me know and we will be friends. If you can't you don't need to bother me, just show yourself out since you know the way."

I dutifully made the call to my senior management at headquarters and explained the situation. To say everyone on the call was in shock was an understatement. Once we snapped out of it, we discussed for about 30 minutes before concluding on a decision—one that we all agreed on. We agreed that, although we could authorize this incredibly low price, we would not. The reasons were clear—we had no connection with the VP of engineering, we had no trust in him, and it was abundantly clear that he did not value the benefits of a long-term relationship. Afterward as I took time to think about this interesting adventure, I realized what had been fundamentally missing was a basic alignment of values, both company-to-company and individual-to-individual. I never did make that sale, but I was happy that I didn't. Values are critically important in life, in business and in sales, so don't ever, ever compromise on them!

"When your values are clear to you,
making decisions becomes easier."
Roy E. Disney

Summary

1. Think about, and be crystal clear on what your own values are; when people ask you about them, don't be wishy-washy!
2. Discovering and aligning with a customer's values can create a lasting connection with them.
3. Alignment of values with your customers can create significant competitive advantage for you.

Remember Only This

"Embrace values, be consistent with them, and take the time to discover them in other people!"

10

Binding Propositions

"Value is what you get!"
Warren Buffett

To sell anything, whether a product, service or even yourself, requires the other person (the buyer) to be interested enough in what is being offered, that they agree to buy from you. It's really that simple. Realizing that it is the interest and commitment of the buyer that is key to complete the sale, then all sales professionals must become masters of ethically convincing them to the benefits of what is being sold. In fact not only the benefits, but more specifically the benefits that are of interest to them, in their current circumstances. Think of yourself as acting like a detective in trying to discover what is important for the buyer, and then transforming this into an offering that is simply unbeatable!

The Unbeatable Value Proposition

Everyone who sells will have a value proposition of some sort or another. Your competition may not always present their value proposition, which if so only makes it easier for you to successfully sell your own. However, most professional salespeople think they know about value propositions, and most believe they are delivering one at every customer opportunity. This unfortunately is not so, since the applicability of a value proposition can only truly be assessed through the eyes of the prospective buyer, and many salespeople (and in fact many companies), do not have a mechanism to test, and periodically retest, their value proposition offerings.

The question now relevant is whether an unbeatable value proposition can be created in the first instance. If so, it becomes the responsibility of the sales professional to find the right prospective customer at the right time, and deliver this value proposition with the energy, enthusiasm and commitment it deserves. Remember the stronger the value proposition through the eyes of the customer, the less "selling" that needs to be done, and in fact it becomes more a process of information exchange.

Creating an unbeatable value proposition is not easy. It takes time, creativity, experience, testing, retesting and ultimately professional delivery in real-world situations. A process can be created that allows all of this to take place in a timely manner, and facilitates a much higher percentage of success with known customer opportunities. However, remember that not all value propositions are good for everyone, no matter how much you think they are. For myself, I love Apple products—I have an iPhone, iPad, MacBook Air for traveling and a large iMac for my office. The value proposition of Apple products is well known. I love to share my Apple experience with friends and colleagues. But even today Apple still has a relatively small share in many markets, since there is significant choice and competition. The value propositions of other competitive solutions have their own unique and special benefits, which seen through the eyes of many buyers, is more superior to Apple's solutions. Customers will therefore make their own decisions, based on their own research that reveals apparent benefits to them. Inputs can come from many different types of marketing sources as well as in-person interactions with sales professionals.

Multiple Value Propositions

It's clear value propositions can be used at different times throughout a typical customer engagement. By communicating certain types of value proposition early on, it can help cement a new relationship, and provide a foundation from which to grow it over time. Consider the following examples of what a professional salesperson will need to develop or have at his disposal:

1. A personal value proposition that allows him to create and maintain amazing connection with the prospective buyer.
2. A company value proposition that highlights both credibility and worthiness of his company, allowing them to appear highly suitable.
3. One or more product or service value propositions that solve real-world problems for customers, and are so compelling that they are chosen over competitive solutions.

Creating Your Unique Personal Value Proposition

With the knowledge that it's essential to create a good first impression, and the fact this is achieved through making a solid connection with the other person, you must start at this early stage of engagement to see things through the eyes of your future customer. Being in sales means it's not about you—at least not initially. It starts with the other person, their company, then you and your company, then your product or service offering. You are merely the conduit through which these things can be communicated. In sales a person's ego can often get in the way—in fact egocentric characteristics can be a ball and chain around the ankle of any professional salesperson. Transitioning to become ego-free (although extremely difficult) will result in truly understanding the world through the eyes of your future customer—making the matching of their challenges and opportunities to your products and services much more possible, and in fact probable. Resist at all costs making the selling process about you!

As an example of how a strong, egocentric personality can get in the way of a sale, I remember working with a highly successful sales professional who had incredible personal drive. He would always take the opportunity of sharing with customers how it was his job to make commission dollars, since he was only on a small base salary, and it was important that he won those commission dollars to "feed his family." He drove an expensive BMW and wore expensive suits and shoes, and always had the latest electronics (phone, laptop, etc.). His words did not seem to be congruent with his appearance—he was talking about feeding his family not buying the latest, flashy gear!

Although he knew the company's value propositions very well, and delivered them very well, he always led with the requirement of "feed my family." Obviously he was earning more than enough to do that, and some! With increasing competition the salesperson began to lose more deals, since he was leading with the wrong thing—he was leading with his requirement to make money and not solving the customer's challenges, or helping them realize their opportunities. Of course over time this strategy brought much attention to his pricing model, which unfortunately came under constant scrutiny by his customers. He did in fact achieve sales in many cases through tenacity and salesmanship, but his profitability for the company became extremely low. He failed to realize that making a connection first, and then delivering a value proposition that was important through the eyes of the customer, was the key starting point of any lasting relationship.

So, for your own personal value proposition, use your skills of connection from the first chapter to create an immediate positive impression that can be built on over time. Make the other person key in this connection rather than yourself. It's quite common and smart to share personal values at this stage since people connect quickly when these are expressed. Seek to find things you both have in common and both value, and you will be off to a great start. Remember to continue to develop connection at a suitable pace with every follow-on interaction. It's this connection strengthening that allows you to easily find out more information that will lead to higher and more profitable levels of sales. Make the communication of your own value proposition part of the initial connection process and see how it directly aids in building deeper and longer-lasting relationships.

Developing Your Compelling Company Value Proposition

When you represent a company, you are in essence being the face of the company through the eyes of the potential customer. They see and experience the company in part through your interactions with them. It is essential therefore to be able to fully explain the value propositions of your company consistently and also have them mesh seamlessly with your own personal value propositions. Having both sets of value propositions integrate well with each other will give the customer great confidence that both you and the company are what you say they are. It's a great starting point to build further connection.

Understanding what makes your company truly unique is essential to create a compelling value proposition. NOTE: One of the most significant ways of differentiating yourself at this early stage is to *create your company value proposition through the eyes of your customer!* Remember to do your research up front on the customer's business, their challenges, their offerings to the market, and their financial goals and performance. Most of this can be found through web-based research or by direct interaction with people who know the customer well. Take the time upfront to do this research and use all the available tools at your disposal including LinkedIn, industry reports, association attendance, press releases, etc. Now begin to authentically mesh this information with your own company information and make it relevant for what's important through your customers' eyes.

Create Your Product or Service Value Propositions

Many people make the mistake of jumping to this stage without first honing their personal and company value propositions. Resist the urge to do so, since the first two value propositions will give you keys in which to be consistent with your product and service value propositions. Remember, the more all three value propositions appear congruent, the more professional and polished you will look, and the easier it will be to connect and ultimately make a sale. There are four steps to consider in constructing a winning product or service value proposition:

Step 1: Collection Phase

The starting point should be the collection of data, facts, marketing material, relevant analysis and projections/forecasts. They should be readily available from various internal resources including marketing, product management, R&D and applications engineering. The goal at this stage is to cast the net wide and capture as much information as possible that may be relevant. Expect it to be in lots of different formats from hardcopy to electronic, and highly presentable all the way through to handwritten notes. Think of these informational pieces as being part of the jigsaw puzzle, and your goal in the following stages is to create a picture that is relevant, appealing and of value to the prospective customer.

Step 2: Benefits Phase

When thinking of benefits, take each piece of data you have from Step 1, and transform it into a benefit. A benefit can be thought of as an advantage, convenience or service conferred to your customer, something that translates the internal language of your company in a way that is both relevant and understood by them. Benefits should be clearly articulated and any assumptions made noted clearly to stop any future ambiguity or misunderstanding.

For example, if you are selling a computer that is twice as fast as the previous generation, then the benefit is not that it can process twice as fast as before (that's the facts), but instead how it relates to the customer's business and confers an advantage, convenience or service to them. Some of these benefits may include reducing costs, increasing productivity, reducing timelines or tackling challenges that were once cost prohibitive. Make these as specific as possible and remember each piece of the jigsaw puzzle can on occasion generate more than one benefit.

Step 3: Differentiated Benefits Phase

Now things start to get interesting! It is clear that most businesses have competition in some form or another. It's not unusual (and in many cases should be expected) that your competitors will have many of the benefits your products and services have. The key to this stage is to identify in a clear, creative, unambiguous and highly authentic way, the things that make you different against your competitors' value propositions. This can be a challenging stage and may require help from the wider internal team, who need to exhibit creativity and understanding of the challenges and opportunities your customers face. This is likely to be an iterative approach, and so don't expect to have it one hundred percent nailed at your first customer interaction—it won't be!

Step 4: End-User Differentiated Benefits Phase

Now you are almost done, but not quite. In my experience this is the stage at which even some of the most talented sales professionals and companies can fall short. They successfully implement the first three steps above, and then fail to capitalize on all the great work, that with a final push can create an unbeatable value proposition! This step requires taking the output of steps 2 and 3 and tailoring it for the individuals at the customer. As an example, you will need to identify who is the buyer, and is there in fact an economic and technical buyer. This includes knowing clearly who will sign-off on the purchase—remember it could be an individual or a team-based decision, so do whatever research is required to build up a clear understanding.

When this is known begin to understand the individual's pain points as well as their opportunities, and also (and sometimes even more importantly) how their role is remunerated and recognized internally. Now gear the output of steps 2 and 3 to these elements, placing less emphasis on the ones that are not so important to them, and instead emphasizing the ones that are important to them. Of course take the opportunity of highlighting how the less important benefits may in fact help others in their company. It's wise to explain you have all the bases covered for the other members of their team as well as them. Having done this you will have created an incredibly compelling value proposition geared exactly to their needs and desires. Of course you may not win the opportunity even with this great work, however if I were a betting man, I would bet you had seriously increased your chances of winning now!

Practicing and Testing—It's a Must!

Now you have what you need (or what you think you need), it's time to practice your value propositions. At first I would suggest you begin to learn them one by one. It's clear that in the middle of a meeting you will not always be given the opportunity of "looking everything up." This shows uncertainty and lack of preparation on your part and will develop doubts quickly in the mind of your customer to the viability of your solutions. So get to know the value propositions one by one, being able to explain their benefits with ease, and develop the skill of bringing up these benefits at the right time in the conversation. Once learned, it's time to put them into practice in the real world. If possible practice with your smaller customer opportunities first, and then migrate up to the larger, more important and impactful customers, as you gain skill in the delivery of your end-user differentiated value propositions.

At this stage expect that you will learn much through the actual delivery phase. When you learn something new, challenge yourself, and if necessary your internal staff, to tweak some of the benefits that will affect the value proposition's effectiveness. By operating with a closed-loop system for feedback and change, you will quickly hone the benefits to deliver a compelling set of reasons why the customer should choose you!

Remember to be careful when you think you have "a perfect set of value propositions." Many a professional salesperson has failed to change, enhance or upgrade their value propositions amongst the many changes that consistently happen in business, including new technology introductions, new competitors, changing industry dynamics, etc. Take heed and consistently and diligently test your value propositions, and always look for ways to make them even stronger. Remember the old saying that "the only constant in life is change itself."

"If you work for money, you'll never make it, but if you love what you're doing and you always put the customer first, success will be yours."
Ray Croc

Summary

1. Data and information are transformed into benefits, and benefits transformed into value propositions when they confer an advantage, convenience or service to your customer. It's that simple!
2. Product and service value propositions are developed through a clear four-step process. Develop the skills necessary for every step, and remember not to make the most common mistake of stopping after completion of Step 3!
3. Value proposition creation is a mind-set that must be mastered by the professional salesperson. It includes personal, company, product and service value propositions, which must all be congruent to each other.

Remember Only This

"See the world through the eyes of your customer!"

THE
INFLUENCING
HABIT

(Sharing Knowledge & Opportunity)

11

Powerfully Influencing

"The greatest ability in business is to get along with others and to influence their actions."
John Hancock

One day when I was early in my sales and marketing career, I attended a really important customer meeting. It was an initial meeting to explore the possibility of the customer using one of the devices offered by the company I was representing. At the start of the meeting, I was so excited that I decided to skip the necessary step of connecting with the Engineering manager. I went straight into "telling" him how good our device was, how bad the competition was, and that if he signed up today he would be able to get some early and scarce samples of our new wonder device.

After I made my pitch, which was short and full of data, the Engineering manager sat back in his chair and said "I am not convinced, so convince me now!" I looked at him in disbelief, not understanding why he did not automatically understand the superiority of our device, and how good it was for him and his company. For a minute I thought he must be joking with me before signing up for the samples. However, he sat quietly, looking intently at me, and waited for me to respond. I had completed a few other similar meetings in Switzerland the week before (my first ever customer meetings) and managed to get both customers to sign up on the day. So what was happening here, and what was so different with this customer compared to the other two?

Fortunately, and through "thinking on my feet," I quickly concluded he was not joking with me, and genuinely wanted to be convinced. Something clicked then and the words "I need to influence him well enough that he will be convinced" came to mind. I knew then that the "convinced" part was actually the outcome I wanted him to reach, and the "influencing" part was what I now had to do to ensure he was fully convinced. I realized I had never actually "influenced" a customer to do something they were not sure about before! And so began my multi-decade quest to learn how best to influence people in a sales situation, but to do so in a way that allowed me to adhere to my own personal values, and still develop a successful sales and management career. So, where to start?

What Really is Influencing?

In sales, apart from the challenging task of prospecting, the fun part of taking orders, and the necessary discipline of management reporting, the biggest, and arguably the most important, part of any sales function is the skill and art of influencing. So what exactly is influencing, and why is it so important for sales professionals to master this?

To fully understand influencing, we need to understand the dynamics of the human mind, especially as it relates to sales and business. People from early in their career are trained to be skeptical, and to seek out as much knowledge as they can about something, before making a decision. This can materialize in lots of different ways, including much online research, a tendency to seek out multiple solutions to a problem, and then comparing each of these possible solutions against one another, and against the customer's perception of their ideal solution. Inevitably questions arise, differences in competing solutions found, and so begins the most important part of the sales professional's function—to convince the customer that their solution is the best through the application of ethical influencing!

In this context influencing can be considered as the process of moving a person's opinion from one state to another, with this new state being the required one that brings them to the point of "being convinced," and of course being convinced in your favor! In today's hypercompetitive sales environment, it's becoming more unusual for potential customers to be convinced immediately, and take their state from a baseline of "not being convinced" to "being completely convinced" without substantial ethical influencing by a sales professional.

Why Do We Need to Influence in the First Place?

Influencing, when done in an ethical way, is a proper and necessary process to help convince a person to change their mind. Their initial stance, or position, might include one or more of the following:

1. A lack of knowledge or understanding of your value proposition, that requires further information.
2. The challenge of obtaining enough information from you, which can then be compared against other competing solutions.
3. A current position that is in favor of a competitive solution.
4. A clear understanding of your current value proposition, that puts the customer in a strong position to ask even more from you.

What is noticeable with many sales professionals is that they do not know which of the four stages their customer resides in at any particular moment in time. Assumptions, as discussed in an earlier chapter, should be completely avoided here, and instead direct questions asked of the customer to determine their current state. Most customers will openly share this information if asked in a genuine and professional way. Again, when an initial connection is made with a customer, they are much more likely to be transparent with you as the process of influencing develops. Remember also their answer to your questions on which state they are in will likely be correct at that point in time, so ask your questions periodically to keep abreast of their evolving status, until such times as they are completely convinced!

It should be noted that influencing is a necessary part of professional salesmanship and should never be considered from a negative perspective. Customers nowadays are predisposed to this requirement, so never go into a meeting with a customer thinking that this part of the sales process is unnecessary and to be avoided. Embrace it, learn the skills and art of influencing, and attain the significant benefits of doing this well.

Are There Different Types of Influencing?

Throughout this chapter, we have referred to ethical influencing and explained its meaning in different ways. Of course, there is also unethical influencing that consists of underhand tactics, which may include the following:

1. **Fear** (of something *important* to the prospective customer).

2. **Threatening** (of something of *value* to the prospective customer).

3. **Withholding** (of something *necessary* for the prospective customer).

4. **Extorting** (of something of *value* to the nonprofessional salesperson).

These underhand tactics can be disguised in such a way by the nonprofessional salesperson to look less than what they really are. Simply put they are unacceptable and improper tactics that don't align with professional salesperson ethics. They should be avoided at all costs; since choosing any of these options will take you down a path that you may ultimately never be able to recover from. Many an aspiring sales career collapsed when news of their underhand tactics were revealed to their management. Take the high road and always choose to influence ethically.

Ten Key Ways to Influence Ethically

There are many ways to reach agreement with a customer that entail *doing the right things at the right time*. Ethical influencing is all about doing exactly this. These are my own top ten favorite examples, but of course there are many more to consider:

1. **Seek to uncover, and deal only in facts:** Resist the urge to draw too many conclusions from assumptions being made. Assumptions should always be verified as soon as possible in a customer interaction. It's absolutely acceptable to ask a business question to a customer, even if you believe it to be a "tough question." The worst they can say to you is "no," or some variation of this.

2. **Build from common ground, strengthening the foundation:** In all influencing discussions there is normally a process that leads to being totally convinced. Taking small steps and getting agreement at each stage helps build the start of a solid foundation. From this foundation more agreement should be added, thus building toward the goal of complete agreement. Resist the urge to try and jump quickly to your desired endpoint without obtaining, and openly accepting the smaller, consensus-building agreements.

3. **Embrace differences of opinion openly:** The biggest challenge people have with ethical influencing is when a disagreement, or simple difference of opinion is encountered. Treat these differences as opportunities to ask more questions, dig a bit deeper, and learn even more about the other person, the customer and the opportunity. With

more questions, solutions can often reveal themselves. If there appears to be a sticking point, note it down and come back to it later, while still striving for momentum towards reaching final agreement. Remember also that on occasion it's absolutely acceptable to have a difference of opinion—agreement on the major topic can often be reached, even with the existence of a small, and potentially not-so-important difference of opinion.

4. **Allow proper time for the influencing process to progress:** It is consistent with ethical influencing that you should never try and rush the process, even at times when you are in a position to do so. People need the right amount of time to digest information, and be able to process information without feeling pressurized to accept. Instead become aware of the process stage the customer is at, and continue to develop toward a satisfactory conclusion without rushing.

5. **Encourage open and constructive debate:** Agreement can normally be reached much faster through ethical influencing when there is a basis of open and constructive debate. If you think something, and then realize it's an assumption, then seek clarification though questioning. Direct or indirect questioning can be used here to unearth and subsequently quash the assumption. Healthy debate should be encouraged since it is extremely likely at the start of any discussion that the customer does not fully agree with your value proposition, or has incomplete information. He may also be making his own assumptions, which might be wholly wrong. Debate in a spirit of partnership can quickly resolve differences and reach consensus faster.

6. **Don't expect to have all the answers immediately:** When debate arises as it naturally will, you will likely find the customer asking questions you may not know the answer

to. Resist the urge to gloss over these questions, or even worse make up answers! This is a complete no-go for ethical influencing. Instead note the questions and get answers from whatever sources are available to you as fast as possible. Once completed, communicate these answers as quickly as possible to the customer. Remember each touch point (communication) you have with a customer that is positive in nature, is helping build up connection, and their confidence in you and your value propositions.

7. **Keep track of what has been agreed to, ideally in writing:** In the middle of a complex negotiation it's often difficult to remember everything that has been agreed, especially when there are multiple variables being discussed. Be disciplined enough to keep track of the agreements, no matter how small, and use this list as a way of periodically summarizing with the customer. This positive re-enforcement helps keep the momentum moving briskly along.

8. **Be truthful, even with unavoidable bad news:** Oftentimes bad news, or at least non-ideal news, will surface. Ethical influencing means sharing information at a time that is proper and right for the customer, and resisting the urge not to communicate it, or choosing to share it near the end of the process. Even worse is when this information is shared after agreement has been reached. One-off deals in sales are good—however consistent, repeatable deals are where true long-term success resides!

9. **Encourage a long-term partnership approach:** Once you have had success with a customer, it's substantially easier to keep them happy, and through this gain further business, compared to starting off the entire sales process of customer identification, customer negotiation, and subsequently reaching customer agreement again. During initial interactions with a new customer always remember the end

goal is to move toward a long-lasting, mutually-beneficial customer or supplier partnership. This approach is the fastest way of building up your base of business, from which to accelerate to even higher sales success.

10. **Be timely in the completion of all actions and communication:** Today there is a significant amount of information contained on the web and customers expect to be able to get information almost immediately. Whenever they ask you for something you don't have, there is an expectation you will react quickly to get the required answers. Don't assume here, but instead ask the customer when they will require a resolution to the action since this manages their expectations professionally. If possible, use the often practiced "under-commit, over-deliver" principle and use it consistently. This consistency and eagerness to fill in the missing blanks for a customer will in of itself positively influence them!

There is more than one way to ethically influence, hence the richness and scope of this key sales skill. After reviewing the points above, consider taking a few minutes and adding to this list with approaches you have used personally, or have seen other people use successfully. Becoming a lifelong student of ethical influencing will, without doubt, build your reputation, allow closer and more sustainable customer relationships, and ultimately bring you more sales success!

Final Thoughts

As way of a final example of ethical influencing, I once worked with a Scottish colleague who was posted to Paris for a few years. He was well known as a consummate negotiator and rejoiced in sharing his many negotiating conquests. However, although most were quite funny, he did adhere to his own clear ethics and used the power of positive influencing in a masterful way. One of his most "famous" stories was going into a bakery in the outskirts of Paris at 4pm one afternoon. He wanted to buy a long baguette of crusty white bread. On asking the price he quickly became aware he only had enough money for half a loaf—and that this bakery only sold full loaves! He started the process of ethically influencing the bakery owner (who had also baked the bread early that morning). My colleague initially chose not to share his financial predicament, but instead explained it was late in the afternoon and it was becoming unlikely the baker would make any money from this particular loaf. Also, he argued that since the bread was baked early in the morning and it was now late afternoon, the bread was no longer as fresh, and then finally he admitted to the baker he only had enough money to buy half a loaf. The shrewd baker, after being ethically influenced and convinced, halved the loaf and started packaging the bread.

My colleague happened to notice that the halving process was not done perfectly, and that he was getting the smaller half of the loaf. Undeterred, and determined to procure the bigger half, he restarted his influencing efforts and shared with the baker the unlikely possibility he would be able to sell the other half of the loaf to a local Parisian at this late hour—especially if it was a shorter half! The outcome was that he did in fact procure the more ideal and larger half loaf at a price he could afford, and both he and the baker shook hands amicably once the baker was convinced. As a thank-you for influencing ethically, the baker also gave my colleague the shorter half of the loaf as way of thanks!

* In case you are wondering about the opening story of this chapter before you read further, I did ultimately influence the Engineering manager successfully, and he did become convinced, but only after 3 hours of deep discussion, and 3 really strong espressos! Patience and coffee work wonders with influencing!

> *"There is no influence like the influence of a habit."*
> **Gilbert Parker**

Joe Connelly

Summary

1. Influencing is a necessary and expected part of most sales transactions, expected both by the professional salesperson and the prospective customer alike.
2. Influencing is both a skill and an art, which can be mastered through study, practice and repetition.
3. When influencing another, influence in a way that you would consider fair and ethical if the roles were reversed.

Remember Only This

"Always influence ethically!"

Igniting Initiative

"Employers and business leaders need people who can think for themselves—who can take initiative and be the solutions to problems."
Stephen Covey

I recall a seasoned sales manager in my early career saying to me "you can choose to do, or you can choose to be told what to do, but whatever option you choose, know it's ultimately your choice!" This piece of sage wisdom was given to me at a time when I was junior enough to expect that my manager would always be telling me what to do. Of course I quickly realized that was not going to happen, and in fact decided to use this to my advantage by trying to do the things that would have the most positive impact for me. And so started the acceleration of my business and sales career through the simple concept of "taking initiative!"

What Exactly is Initiative?

There are numerous definitions to help us understand initiative. I have listed three, which help explain what it is, or can be, in the life of a professional salesperson:

1. The ability to assess and initiate things independently.
2. The power, or ability, to act or take charge before others do.

3. An act, or strategy, designed to resolve a difficulty, or improve a situation; a fresh approach.

It's clear that taking initiative is an inherently positive act, and in fact a positive act of action. Initiative implies taking action, and getting things done proactively. In many ways initiative can also be considered to be the opposite of procrastination, since one encourages action while the other discourages it. Initiative is driven by needs, wants, desires, goals and visions, and somehow helps create enough inertia to overcome the threshold of inaction. Everyone has the ability to ignite initiative, and in fact have done so many times throughout their life. When there is enough incentive to excite and motivate you, know that initiative will surely follow.

For the professional salesperson, initiative is paramount to success. Selling, by its very nature, is a proactive process that requires continuously taking positive action to promote your product or service to your customer base, and then convincing them to buy it. The more initiative a salesperson can take, the higher the likelihood of their sales success—it's that simple!

Initiative and Energy

There is a direct correlation between initiative and personal energy. In many ways one can drive the other, and vice versa, and it's also noteworthy that both positively feed off each other. It's clear having more personal energy seems to give you more confidence to take initiative in the first place, and by taking positive initiative it can generate incremental amounts of personal energy which will generate increased confidence. To create the momentum necessary to achieve your goals, you will need to take positive initiative, and have the energy on tap to carry you toward completion of them. Think of initiative as being the rocket fuel for your action taking!

Also, it's clear the higher you set your goals, the more initiative is required to achieve them, so there is also a direct correlation between "thinking big" and the level of initiative required to "win big."

Why is Initiative Really Necessary?

When an action appears, or a goal is decided upon, the next step is to figure out who is going to complete the action, attain the goal, and by what means. At this stage an individual can choose to wait and be told what to do (the opposite of initiative), or can take it upon themselves to determine what now needs to be done, and simply go do it. Without initiative everybody would be waiting on somebody, and the end result is that nothing would ever get done! Initiative fuels action, and action fuels the achievement of goals and their outcomes.

In sales, customers are rarely queuing at your door waiting to buy your products. In fact if this happens I would say it is not really selling, and much more transacting, since there is no real "selling process" taking place. However, most sales situations require the sales professional to proactively take action, and using whatever means available to him, progress the sale. There will always be a natural resistance to slow things down through normal delays, obstacles and challenges, and initiative must be consistently employed to ensure positive, forward momentum.

Also, there appears to be a direct correlation with initiative and creativity. By taking positive initiative, your creativity and ability to problem-solve will naturally increase. I commonly refer to this sequence of events as the "upward spiral": positive thinking, leading to igniting initiative, leading to breakthrough creativity, leading to accelerated action and thus hyper-performance outcomes.

What Can Stop Initiative in its Tracks?

Everyone will encounter times in their sales career when things simply just don't go as planned. One of the obvious and immediate checks should be to ask what is in your control, and what is not. If something is within your control, it normally implies the need for you to ignite initiative and through this kick-start action. As part of this personal check, you may identify elements that are stopping you from taking personal initiative. Some examples might include:

1. **Fear:** When you are afraid of the outcome, or the actions required to achieve the outcome, it can prove debilitating and stop initiative from igniting, which directly stops ACTION!

2. **Laziness:** We all suffer from laziness at times. Whether it's because we have worked so hard, or maybe because we are having a normal (human) bout of laziness, know that it will work directly against taking initiative.

3. **Procrastination:** The tendency to push action off to a later date (or potentially forever) is the direct opposite of taking positive initiative. Overcoming procrastination will positively impact your ability to take initiative when needed.

4. **Excuse making** is just a way to ensure that you don't have to ignite initiative. It's a way to create reasons why something will go wrong, will be too difficult to achieve, or any manner of reasons that again are convincing you to NOT TAKE ACTION!

5. **Illness** is a natural occurrence for all of us whether it's catching a cold or the flu, or even worse, being stuck in hospital. Illnesses and accidents do happen, and normally at the most unexpected, and inopportune times. My advice here—pay heed and take some much needed quality rest!

6. **Tiredness** is normal and just makes it increasingly harder to kick-start initiative. It may not totally stop it from happening, but realize that it will "feel" much harder to overcome the resistance that will now be holding you back.

The good news is the majority of these examples can be overcome by the eager sales professional who is willing to learn, change, and follow the guidance in this book! Now there may also be reasons outside of your control that stop or discourage taking initiative. If that is the case, then be wise and know this is likely understandable. Accept these things and instead invest your available energy thinking of ways that you can take positive initiative. Some examples that might cause initiative to be out of your control are:

1. **Rules and regulations:** Whether there are company regulations, industry legislation, or even the law of the country, know that it's wise to accept these for what they are—things you should NOT BREAK!

2. **Implied expectations:** If customers expect things to be done in a certain way, and you decide to bypass or counteract their guidance, know that you are risking potentially as much as you are gaining through your decision.

3. **Industry or social norms:** As an example, if the normal process for submitting a government work order is clear, then don't try to be clever and bypass it by taking initiative. Stick with the norms, or at least double-check with the customer first if you are going to do something substantially different.

4. **You work in a micromanaged environment:** If you find yourself in this position, you may well be required to do exactly what is being asked of you. However, in my experience there is not a sales job of any sort, which does not rely to some degree or another, on personal initiative. Be bold and apply it!

Things that Discourage Personal Initiative

It's wise to understand what roadblocks there might be that would discourage personal initiative, since this can provide much guidance to stop them from negatively influencing initiative in the first place. For example, you may choose to wait for others to complete actions, or simply choose to delay completion of your own actions. You may also downgrade your visions and goals, and thus have less need to take initiative to advance them. Or, you may simply try and delegate so as not to tackle the action yourself. This last example is potentially acceptable if you are coming from a place of taking initiative, rather than coming from a place of fear or laziness of starting the action.

Potential Downsides of Personal Initiative

With all things positive, if carried through to extremes, they can become detrimental to achieving success. Without doubt the biggest potential downside in taking personal initiative (and especially in a sales function), is loading yourself up with too many actions, and not being able to complete them with enough quality and timeliness. My experience has shown that this was one of my own personal Achilles heels, and it literally has taken me decades to resolve. Even now, my tendency is to say I will do something by applying positive initiative, and then figuring out the time and effort implications later! Also by taking this approach you can often take positive pressure off your peers or team, since they know that historically you have "stepped up to the bar," and when a new action is identified within the team, then you will likely accept it!

Remember that initiative if used unwisely, can become a big ball and chain, and really slow down your overall sales progress, which of course is exactly the opposite of what you are hoping it will do. Know that taking initiative means accepting actions, and those actions need to be transposed into your calendar with the right time and priority allocation to do them justice. By managing your calendar well you can choose when to ratchet up, or ratchet down your personal initiative!

Consequences of Not Taking Initiative

If you have been in sales for a while now, you will know it is a highly competitive environment, and in fact always has been. Your competitors are constantly trying to win new business, or trying to prize away the business you currently have. Also, within a sales team there can be lots of pressures to perform against your peers, and keep yourself away from the "cut-off list." It is often said there is nowhere to hide in sales—you either bring in the revenues and profit, or you don't! It's crucial therefore to show initiative within your own team, with your customers, as well as any other stakeholders you are engaged with. These stakeholders could include board members, your extended sales channel, press, partners, associations, or even in some rare cases your competition. By choosing not to take suitable initiative when required, you are accepting at least "second best", and in many cases you may be choosing "least best". You should never plan to be last in any sales endeavor, and in fact the only way to truly thrive is to shoot for "first best" at all times. You may not always achieve it, but you will surely win more than your fair share with this more positive, and initiative-driven approach.

Key Sales Skills to Ignite Initiative

Without doubt one of the biggest challenges you will encounter as a professional salesperson, is what to do if you feel your initiative is not strong enough, or you are not using it often enough to achieve your business goals. This is a tough one indeed, since initiative happens at such an early stage in the sales process, that without it, progress can be severely impacted or even halted. I have seen many good salespeople leave their sales career due solely to "not wanting to constantly push and take initiative." I have also seen a very direct correlation between hyper-performing salespeople and the amount of initiative they are willing to take, day-in and day-out. So what can be done to nurture and develop personal initiative and so achieve this hyper-performance? Consider some of these examples, and also see if you can add a few more from your own experiences:

1. **Dream really, really big:** By setting your goals and aspirations really high, you automatically frame the future in a much more positive and exciting light. This will naturally cause more initiative to be taken toward attaining your big dream.

2. **Surround yourself with like-minded individuals:** It's often said that you can ascertain much about a person by knowing who their friends and close colleagues are. Choose wisely here, and ensure you quickly weed out people who don't share your positive and optimistic outlook on life.

3. **Get into a positive routine:** This will help de-clutter your mind, and allow space for creativity and intuition. Allowing your mind to fill with such positive things will also trigger initiative and positive risk-taking.

4. **Employ a coach or mentor:** But make sure they are good at what they do. A good coach will always gently nudge you to operate slightly out of your comfort zone, edging up your sales performance surely and consistently.

5. **Work for a truly great company, or for yourself:** There is a raw energy created when working for yourself, being your own boss, and the master of your own destiny. This often encourages initiative in a person, and many people have risen to great heights by choosing this route. Being your own boss will undoubtedly involve a very high degree of selling skills, and not only to customers. The other alternative is to work for a great, positive thinking "can do" company, since there is a team energy that can quickly

be tapped into, to encourage confidence and personal initiative.

6. **Develop challenging hobbies outside of work:** This will also directly encourage initiative, but this time related to a fun and exciting hobby. Once initiative is ignited in your hobby, it becomes easier to embrace it in your sales role.

7. **Become a student of sales teachings:** You will come across lots of inspiring stories of how sales professionals, just like you, applied initiative, continued to learn and grow, and developed a truly successful and rewarding sales career. Become a lifelong student, develop deep curiosity and remember to read lots!

It should be abundantly clear now that igniting initiative, and great sales performance, go hand-in-hand. Take time to develop your initiative to the point where you consider it "best in class" and you will surely end up being just that!

Put Yourself Out There

As a final thought on igniting initiative, I recall a story of when I was working as a VP of sales in Canada. One of my staff recounted a story to me that was both simple and brilliant at the same time. She was based in the company's Canadian headquarters, and trying to contact one of her customers who was based in the United States. She had tried many times, but with no luck. Eventually she managed to get hold of the Procurement manager, and he quickly dismissed her by saying he was really swamped with work and under lots of time pressure to get some key deliverables to his supervisor. In fact he also said, "It's so bad I don't even have time to get a coffee!" Not to be deterred by this obstacle, the Sales director searched on Google and found the location of the nearest Starbucks to the customer's premises. She called them, ordered a coffee, and then separately called for a taxi to deliver the coffee promptly to the customer, all paid on her personal credit card. All of this was done within ten minutes of the customer call, and the coffee delivered to his office shortly thereafter.

The same day the Sales director received a surprise thank-you call from the customer. Needless to say she had done an amazing job, taking positive initiative, and quickly developed a powerful connection with the customer. It is safe to say that she did in fact get lots of business from the customer, and also the knowledge her calls would now be answered or returned in a timely manner! Initiative that knew no bounds—simply brilliant!

"Hold up a mirror and ask yourself what you are capable of doing, and what you really care about. Then take the initiative—don't wait for someone else to ask you to act."
Sylvia Earle

Summary

1. Understanding and taking initiative is the lifeblood of being in sales, and truly igniting initiative will, over time, become a key differentiator in your career.
2. Choosing to ignite initiative brings with it so many other significant benefits, including increased positivity, heightened creativeness, and also higher energy reserves to simply get more done.
3. Learn to have complete control over your personal initiative, and realize that there are times to really apply it, and times to keep it in reserve until you are time-balanced once more.

Remember Only This

"Initiative is your rocket fuel for action taking!"

THE
BALANCING
HABIT

(Manifesting Lasting Success)

13

Balance Mastery:
The Sales Habit Way

*"It's all about quality of life and finding a happy balance
between work and friends and family."*
Philip Green

I remember a very poignant story to highlight the pitfalls of not having balance in life. When I was younger and moved into my first apartment at the grand old age of 27, I met my new neighbors. I became friendly with Jim and Grace who were both 65 years of age, quite wealthy and who were eagerly looking forward to a long and happy retirement. When I got to know them a bit better, they explained how hard they had worked since they were 16 years of age. Jim started working in a butcher's shop and later saved enough money to start his own business. He later met Grace; they got married and became a great husband and wife partnership in business, and in life. Their success grew over the years and they developed the business well enough to own five very busy shops in the local area.

They owned a huge house they spent very little time in. They were so busy they could not afford the time for vacations or much relaxation. Weekends were busiest with customers, and the week was always steady business and then getting prepared for the weekend rush. Special occasions like Christmas and New Year were even busier since customers always wanted more with additional special orders. Jim and Grace accumulated lots of money, and lots of stress. When they both retired at 65 they quickly downsized to a small apartment, sold their business, and got ready to have a wonderful retirement. 6 months later Jim died of a heart attack, and 12 months later Grace took a physically debilitating stroke and had no option but to go into long-term managed care.

I had just experienced my first true lesson on life imbalance! Since then, although I can honestly say I have not always practiced balance in my own life, and in fact many times have been completely out of balance, this was an essential lesson for me!

What Exactly is Balance?

Balance is a completely personal thing, viewed differently by different people. What works for one person may be very different from what works for another. In many ways balance is what you think and want it to be. As an example, if you look forward to later years and think of your retirement, some people want to immediately stop working and travel the world, some leave work and stay close at home, while others say they will continue to work. You see, everyone has an opinion and that in the end is what counts with balance. What is clear though, is that whatever your opinion of balance is in your life, it's wise to move toward this ideal, sustaining position as fast as possible. But why?

Balance is a very complex subject for sales professionals, and in fact everyone. It involves your mind, body and spirit. Realizing that sales in particular is a physically, mentally, emotionally and spiritually demanding profession, what are the benchmarks you should consider setting yourself, irrespective of what balance ultimately looks like for you?

1. **Physically** keeping yourself active enough to de-stress from the many pressures of being in sales. Activity, especially activity that raises your heartbeat, is fun, and allows you to participate in at least three times per week, will give you in return, even more energy to keep you at your sales peak throughout your career. Couple this with getting the right

amount of sleep, no matter how many meetings you have, how much travel you are doing, or how many e-mails you have to wrestle with. And of course eating and drinking what you instinctively know is good for you. Just listening to your inner voice is guide enough for most people. So are you exercising enough, sleeping enough and eating and drinking well enough? If you are doing all these things well right now, then know that you are automatically in the Top 1% of all sales professionals, and have given yourself a real, long-term sustainable advantage over your competition!

2. **Mentally** challenging yourself is one of the joys (and challenges) of being in sales. There is always something happening that will test you mentally and really get you thinking. Whether it's how to construct a complex sales proposal, how to ethically influence someone, or how to get the most out of your limited time, you will likely find that your mind is incredibly active from the minute you arise in the morning to when you collapse in bed at night! But do you take the time to mentally relax, to give your huge brain, this incredible processing engine, time to be still? As your sales career, similar to your life, becomes more complex, this stillness becomes harder to achieve, but at the same time increasingly more necessary. Meditation and yoga are two of the best ways of quieting the mind, but even if these don't interest you, or you think you don't have the time for them, then know you do have the time to take small power breaks by yourself to simply relax. What's clear, however, is that whatever you are working on will still be there after your power break! Consider taking at least two small power breaks per day—I recommend one in the morning and one in the afternoon. Fifteen minutes is ideal and everyone can find two slots per day if they try. Go for a walk outside in the fresh air, or sit quietly by yourself and enjoy a cup of coffee or tea. It sounds simple, but trust me when I say it really works!

3. **Emotionally** recharging yourself to handle the demands of an intensive sales career. Learn ways of handling rejection in your role and being able to bounce back from lost or missed opportunities. Become open to criticism in whatever form it arrives, and try and take at least one nugget of wisdom from it—most criticism, even the unfair variety, can often contain a grain of truth that can be positively acted upon. Learn the skills of emotional empathy since human beings are emotional creatures at heart, and a strong relationship can be made and cultivated through emotionally connecting. Remember also to live your business and personal life in alignment with your values, as this will have a direct bearing on your emotional fortitude. Realize also that being human will bring with it both the highs and lows of life, and you will need to tap into your emotional reserve at such times. Last and certainly not least, don't be afraid to positively show your emotions when appropriate. When I was early in my career I was trained not to show emotion, especially during sales negotiations with customers or partners. This approach inevitably spread throughout all of my early interactions. Over the years as I gained more maturity and wisdom, I realized that exhibiting emotions shows you are human and better able to relate and connect with other people. Well-displayed emotions can accelerate the building of relationships and business alike!

4. **Spiritually** boosting yourself is necessary for sales professionals since much of the job is hunting, hitting rejection, and often seems like pushing a big rock uphill. As you encounter the normal challenges, rejections and disappointments that all sales professionals encounter, you will need a way to spiritually recharge and get yourself ready to tackle the next day. All great athletes have ways of recharging their spirit, even after significant loss in competitions. Dreaming, visualizing and journaling are all ways of reflecting on what is happening in your life, trying

to put it in order and ultimately allowing you the time and space to connect with your subconscious. Through this you can also connect with the amazing life force that resides both within, and all around you. Sales professionals frequently encounter more disappointments than most professions, and need to pay particular attention to their spirituality. Know for sure that great sales professionals seem to have an endless reservoir of spirituality from which they draw on as times need, giving them the confidence and understanding that success comes to those who stay positive!

It is clear that some people can be quite successful in sales by living their life out of balance. They allocate more time to their career, do whatever it takes, whenever it is required, and simply use raw personal horsepower to muscle their way to success. But the question that must be asked is "to what end"? Success in one area of your life does not mean you automatically achieve life success. As I get older, and now have more examples from which to draw my own conclusions, I see clearly that the sales professionals I consider to be most successful are the ones who have the best combination of life balance, and through this are evidently the happiest! In fact my next book entitled *The Holistic Executive*, is all about the amazing power that life balance can have on business performance. For me balance is the missing link, the Holy Grail for all professionals!

The Serious Outcomes of Imbalance

As the introductory story highlighted there are serious outcomes of living your life out of balance. Everything from poor sales performance, ill health, compromised relationships, divorce, all the way to simply missing out on the many joys of life. These outcomes, as well as a long list of others, are serious enough to warrant your close attention and reflection. Know that if any area of your life is out of balance it will affect your sales performance to some degree or other. Strive for life balance, and through this you will begin to see your own sales performance improve. For me personally, this was one of my toughest lessons to learn, and has caused many personal challenges and sacrifices over the years. However, I believe I have cracked it now, and I can tell you, it really is worth fighting for!

Top Habit-Forming Tips to Achieve Balance

Being in sales is a constant struggle, a constant effort, and a constant challenge, to hit or exceed your revenue targets. It takes great courage, great energy and great perseverance to stay the course and develop a balanced, healthy and ultimately rewarding sales career. Balance in sales as in life can be an elusive thing. I see so many people who don't have balance in their careers or lives, and choose to blame any of a number of factors (there is a whole chapter dedicated to this in Chapter 4 "Extinguishing Excuses"). In addition to the tips above on physical, mental, emotional and spiritual balance, listed below are my favorite coaching tips for key sales characteristics and skills that can, and should, be developed to attain true-life balance, and through this exceptional sales mastery.

Six Key Characteristics of Sales Balance

Consider these six key characteristics and try and add a few of your own to truly re-enforce and instill the importance of balance in your life:

1. **Courage** to enter and stay in the challenging, but ultimately rewarding, world of professional sales. The courage to challenge yourself to operate outside of your comfort zone, since it's in this zone that accelerated learning and success reside.
2. **Motivation** to keep going through the natural up's and down's of the sales process. By taking a longer-term perspective on sales, you will begin to see with every situation you encounter, something positive can be

The 6 Sales Habits

taken from it. As Napoleon Hill famously noted in his inspirational book *Think and Grow Rich,* "Every apparent defeat has contained within it the seed of an equivalent or greater benefit." Stay motivated and go seed hunting!

3. **Energy-conscious thinking** is becoming more understood as scientists and philosophers begin to align positive thinking and success to energy. In sales, as in life, try to pass on positive energy through *doing the right things at the right time*, and in so doing you will attract more of the same. The pool of energy from which we can all draw from, is, as we all instinctively know, infinite!

4. **Strategic thinking** to help visualize what your intermediate and end goals are, and to enable you to use the vast resources of your brain to formulate the best, most productive, most efficient and most expedient way of achieving your desired success. Strategic thinking elevates you above the tree line, to see where you are heading and what needs to be overcome to get there.

5. **Discipline** to build a pattern for sales success. Whether it's starting off your morning with meditation or exercise, or completing and submitting your sales expenses in a timely manner, discipline builds character, repetition and ultimately positive, sustaining habits!

6. **A sense of humor** to be your biggest ally against the disappointing, challenging and frustrating things that will challenge you day-in and day-out. Don't take them too seriously, and as with all things they will pass in their own good time and become simply something that was. Laughing creates endorphins, which make you feel better, gives you renewed energy when needed most, and is also incredibly and positively contagious. Laugh out loud, and more often—the world needs it!

Six Key Skills of Sales Balance

Now consider these six key skills and again try and add a few of your own, to really impress the importance of balance in life:

1. **Planning:** is a skill that is necessary to maximize your time and subsequent sales output. It allows you to find the time to organize yourself, think about what is coming up, and wrestle with both challenges and solutions alike. It also, when done wisely, can be used to visualize success and create your future history!

2. **Bouncing back:** is a key skill that can and must be learned quickly in sales. Everyone loses deals and opportunities, and everyone stumbles over road bumps that slow us down. Customers may choose not to like you, not to call you back, or simply to award business to a competitor. Whatever happens learn the skill of bouncing back, and as quickly as possible. Even when losing the biggest of opportunities, do what you need to do to recommit and reenergize, and never let the disappointment spill into the next day—ever!

3. **Recharging:** is a requirement that entails boosting your energy whenever required. It can be a need for a midday energy boost, or the desire for a great night's sleep, all the way to taking two weeks of quality, uninterrupted vacation. Whatever it is that your body and mind are suggesting, listen carefully to your internal voice, since more than likely it will be one hundred percent correct!

4. **Outside interests:** can develop a great way of getting you away from all things sales and giving you more access and enjoyment to other areas of life. What is interesting and intriguing at the same time, is that by doing this, solutions to your sales challenges often come to you apparently "out

of the blue." Remember that Sir Isaac Newton discovered gravity while resting under an apple tree!

5. **Relaxing/quiet times:** are a must to take stock of everything that is happening both in your sales and personal life. Finding quiet time especially, allows you to tune into the great energy force that seems to hold wisdom, motivation, and in fact just about all things, that you will need to be a successful, professional salesperson!

6. **Giving back:** is one of the most rewarding things to do in life. Give back in ways that you can and as often as possible. Whatever it is you choose, do so in a spirit of thanks and appreciation for what you have in your life, and do so without expectation of receiving anything in return. The reality is you will receive back in ways you may not immediately understand, and it will be to a much higher degree. Be bold and do something wonderful for someone today!

Sales habit mastery is a real and achievable potential for those willing to work for it. Balance is without doubt the key to true sales mastery. Create balance in your life, have fun, and see just how successful your sales career can become!

> *"The key is taking responsibility and initiative, deciding what your life is about and prioritizing your life around the most important things."*
> **Stephen Covey**

Summary

1. Balance is worthy of the effort it takes to achieve it.
2. Balance is without doubt a competitive advantage you have against all those salespeople who choose not to have it in their lives.

3. Balance will allow you to become a more complete person, enjoying success in all aspects of your life and not just in your sales career.

Remember Only This

"Balance, and through this happiness, is the ultimate goal of sales habit mastery!"

APPENDICES

Appendix A:
Testing Sales Habit Mastery

*"I am forever testing myself. As a person and as an actor,
I have no sense of competition."*
Michael Caine

Now you have read this book, you can begin to test your understanding (and implementation) of the key concepts and ideas. By doing this you will discover what you know, and what you have now embedded into your own sales approach. Sales mastery takes time and practice and there is no single route to get there. In fact, I have chosen not to give answers to these thought-provoking questions, since there is never just one correct answer. Instead use these questions as little mind puzzles that will get you thinking about your knowledge, your approach, and what skills might still be missing for you. You can refer back to these questions time and again as your sales career develops, to highlight the consistent progress you will undoubtedly be making.

You will know you have achieved sales habit mastery once you can answer each of the questions in an automatic way, without having to search too long in your memory. And also, that each of the questions resonate with you easily, and your answers solid enough to be to your complete satisfaction. Enjoy the mind puzzles, they're tasty treats!

Chapter 1:
The Connection Key

Q1. Do you always choose to CONNECT with someone when you meet them for the first time?

Q2. Do you have well-developed connections with all your current customers and opportunities?

Q3. Do you consistently think about further developing connection with your customers, seeking opportunities to do so with every interaction?

Q4. Are there contacts you have that could be further developed, and a stronger relationship realized, by investing more time connecting with them?

Q5. Do you rate (or measure) the strength of your connection with key customers?

Q6. Are you investing enough time to develop and maintain connection with internal members of your team and company?

Q7. Do you still make assumptions about your contacts, opportunities or customers?

Q8. Have you mastered the skill of unearthing assumptions made by your customers?

Q9. Would you consider yourself to be a great storyteller, pulling from a wide variety of personal stories, and able to use the right one on the right occasion?

Q10. Do you practice using the *Dual Mind*, the *Three Brains*, the *Assumptionator*, the *Storyteller*, and the *Silencer* to aid building connection?

Chapter 2:
Building Teamwork

Q1. Are you currently working with multiple teams?

Q2. Are you currently the team lead for one of more of these teams?

Q3. Do you automatically introduce internal teams to your customers?

Q4. Do you currently have any teams that include direct customer representation?

Q5. Do you routinely celebrate successes, both during, and at the end of a team's life?

Q6. Are you considered, both internally and externally, as a great team player?

Q7. Do you automatically consider teaming as a solution for the majority of actions and challenges that arise?

Q8. Do you actively consider other options to teaming to determine what option is the best in a given situation?

Q9. Do you actively consider the six-key steps of the team building process, when you decide a teaming approach is best?

Q10. Are you still amazing at getting actions done quickly and efficiently yourself, when required?

Chapter 3:
Removing Fears

Q1. Do you still have the same lingering fears you have had for many years?

Q2. Do you always seem to develop a new fear, or set of fears, to replace the ones that are no longer holding you back?

Q3. Do you periodically check-in to see what, if any, fears you might still have?

Q4. Whenever a fear enters your mind, do you immediately become curious about it, stay calm, and ultimately let it dissipate?

Q5. Are there certain common catalysts in your life that always seem to re-energize old fears you have had?

Q6. Can you eradicate a fear from forming and embedding in your mind quickly, by using both the *Fear-Accepting Program* and the *Fear-Removing Program*?

Q7. Have you eradicated the most common sales fears you once had?

Q8. Can you immediately recognize in other people when they start talking about, or exhibiting, fears?

Q9. Do you regularly try and help people who exhibit fears in their personal or working lives?

Q10. Are you confident enough to say you have mastered your fears well enough that you could now coach on the subject?

Chapter 4:
Extinguishing Excuses

Q1. Are you immediately aware the moment you start making an excuse?
Q2. Are you immediately aware the moment someone else starts making an excuse?
Q3. When you start making an excuse do you realize this is actually an outcome to something underlying it, and then seek out what that might be?
Q4. Do you automatically try and unearth the real underlying reasons when a customer makes an excuse?
Q5. Have you changed your daily language to remove the word "problem" and replace it with the word "challenge"?
Q6. Have you burned your own personal copy of *The Book of Excuses*?
Q7. Do you practice the many options to excuse-making, drawing from different options for different situations?
Q8. Do you immediately get angry, or show compassion, when other people make excuses?
Q9. Have you ever counted the amount of excuses you hear in a typical workday?
Q10. Does the making of excuses by other people bring you down in any way?

Chapter 5:
Busting Procrastination

Q1. Have you been resisting reading this Appendix for a while now?
Q2. Do you believe you have stopped all examples of procrastination in your business life?
Q3. Have you implemented a daily check-in to try and uncover if you are currently procrastinating about anything?
Q4. Can you recognize procrastination immediately in other people?
Q5. Have you ever procrastinated about something and ended up with a positive outcome?

Q6. Have you developed a personal planning process that allows you to action the "big rocks" early in your day?

Q7. Do you notice any differences in your approach to procrastination in your personal and business lives?

Q8. Do you fully understand the close linkage between procrastination and fear?

Q9. Have you ever considered the direct linkage between procrastinating and using time inefficiently?

Q10. Have you seen a direct performance improvement, and incrementally better results, by reducing or eliminating procrastination in your sales career?

Chapter 6:
Mastering Time

Q1. Do you keep track and measure the time you spend across the various time buckets?

Q2. Do you keep track and measure the time you allocate to certain activities in your work life?

Q3. Do you intuitively feel as though you are time-balanced in your life?

Q4. Do you reallocate time to a bucket if you have taken from it the previous week?

Q5. Do you feel you have enough time in your life to achieve your business and life goals?

Q6. How many times per day do you check e-mail?

Q7. Do you time block activities in your calendar weekly?

Q8. Do you regularly "have meetings with myself" by blocking off quiet time?

Q9. Do you run with one system for your calendar and actions, and ensure all actions have the right duration and priority?

Q10. Do you periodically investigate *The 80/20 Rule* in your work life to determine if acceleration opportunities are possible?

Chapter 7:
Creating Momentum

Q1. Do you fully understand the concept of leverage?

Q2. Do you continually look for ways of using leverage to accelerate results, or reduce expended effort?

Q3. Is your sales career moving at a speed that is fast enough for you to achieve your longer-term goals and vision?

Q4. Do you have both a business and personal strategy that is documented, referred to regularly, and changes very little?

Q5. Do you actively accept synchronicities into your life (these are the coincidences you decide to take action on)?

Q6. Do you continuously look for more efficient ways of doing the things you have to do frequently?

Q7. Do you instinctively check to see what frictions you have in your life that are slowing down your momentum?

Q8. Before you rush into an action, do you take a moment to determine if there is any leverage possible?

Q9. Do you choose to do something every day (no matter how small) for the achievement of your business and life goals?

Q10. Are you laughing often enough in your life?

Chapter 8:
Manifesting Synchronicities

Q1. Do you actively think about every coincidence that happens in your life?

Q2. Do you notice when coincidences are happening more frequently than at other times?

Q3. Are you clear that taking positive and affirmative action on coincidences can manifest synchronicities?

Q4. Are you clear on the connection between positive thinking and coincidences appearing?

Q5. Are you skeptical about synchronicities in any way?

Q6. Do you actively look for the right action to take once a coincidence is made known to you?

Q7. Can you catch yourself starting to think negatively when everything seems to be going well for you?

Q8. Do you understand that coincidences come in waves, and happen periodically?

Q9. Do you write down coincidences and synchronicities to reflect on them later?

Q10. Do you believe that your life needs to include hardship?

Chapter 9:
Selling Values

Q1. Are you really clear on, and can write down, your own personal values?

Q2. Are you comfortable knowing that you live your business life in full accordance with your values?

Q3. Do you ever find you have to compromise with any of your personal or business values?

Q4. Are you actively transparent with your business dealings, especially with customers?

Q5. Do you tend to "bend the values rules" if you have a very difficult customer to manage, or lucrative opportunity to close?

Q6. Do you believe you know the personal values of the people closest to you?

Q7. Are you consciously trying to unearth values in your customers?

Q8. Do you know all of your customers' company values?

Q9. Have you managed to weave together both your own personal values and those of your company in a synergistic way?

Q10. Are you comfortable sharing, discussing, and even debating values in business?

Chapter 10:
Binding Propositions

Q1. Do you choose to see the majority of business situations through the eyes of your customers to gain possible insights?

Q2. Are you clear on what your personal value proposition is, and do you choose to actively share it with customers?

Q3. Are you clear on what your company value propositions are, and do you consistently and proactively share them with all representatives at your customer base?

Q4. Do you still predominantly talk to customers about data and information, as opposed to benefits they can accrue from this information?

Q5. Do you have clear and compelling value propositions for the products and services you are offering to your customers?

Q6. Are all your value propositions (personal, company, products and services) congruent with each other?

Q7. How, and how often, do you test your value propositions to ensure they remain both appealing and competitive through the eyes of the customer?

Q8. Do you clearly think about discovering the differentiated end-user benefits specific to your customers?

Q9. Do you proactively ask your customers if the value propositions you communicate are what they are looking for?

Q10. Do you occasionally shy away from communicating your personal value propositions to senior staff at customers?

Chapter 11:
Powerfully Influencing

Q1. Do you always choose to influence ethically?

Q2. Do you choose to influence others the way you would find acceptable if the roles were reversed?

Q3. Are you a student of finding new and better ways of ethically influencing people?

Q4. Do you proactively and consistently take time to review scenarios if you did not win an opportunity, and note what you learned for future use?

Q5. Are you comfortable in knowing that most customers will need to be ethically influenced to change their opinion/decision state?

Q6. Do you regularly and proactively check in with customers during the selling phase to see what stage of the decision-making process they are in?

Q7. Do you actively list assumptions you, or your customers, are making and then find ways to quash them one by one?

Q8. Are you ever aware of a customer trying to influence you in an unethical manner, and if so, are you clear how to handle this?

Q9. Are you accepting of different opinions from customers, even when they are very different from your own?

Q10. Have you mastered the "say/do gap"—doing exactly what you said you would do, in all circumstances?

Chapter 12:
Igniting Initiative

Q1. Are you happy with the current level of initiative shown toward your sales career?

Q2. Can you turn up, or turn down, your initiative at will?

Q3. Do you fully understand all the benefits of igniting your initiative?

Q4. Do you fully understand the codependency of initiative and personal energy?

Q5. Can you immediately spot whatever might be trying to slow down, or stop, your initiative materializing?

Q6. Do you know when to use your initiative and when to simply play by the rules?

Q7. Can you readily control your initiative so as not to become action overloaded?

Q8. Do you consistently dream of the attainment of really big sales goals?

Q9. Do you have people in your direct sphere who negatively draw energy and excitement from you?

Q10. Do you regularly push out of your comfort zone and feel happy in this state?

Chapter 13:
Balance Mastery: The Sales Habit Way

Q1. Are you aware of the personal feelings and dynamics felt when you are in life balance?

Q2. Are you aware of the personal feelings and dynamics felt when you are not in life balance?

Q3. Do you intuitively and intellectually believe that life balance is a competitive advantage in your career?

Q4. Do you have ways of checking for balance in your personal life, for example, asking your partner?

Q5. Do you regularly find that solutions to complex business challenges come to you when you are most relaxed?

Q6. Are you really clear what balance means for you, and when you are in, or out, of balance?

Q7. How long are you willing to operate out of balance, before making necessary changes?

Q8. Do you eat, drink, sleep and exercise the way you intuitively know is right for you?

Q9. Do you find ways of resting your mind and giving yourself quality time to relax, recover, and recharge?

Q10. Do you have methods and techniques to boost your spirit when needed to keep you at the top of your game?

Appendix B:
Key Concepts Summary

If you are like me, once you have read a book, especially one with lots of tips, tricks, and thought-provoking ideas, having to summarize the key ones can seem daunting. To help, I have captured in the following pages the points that will become a ready-reckoner for you (in essence a short, management summary).

Everything detailed in this book, and in this key concepts summary section, are real world, tried-and-tested ideas that simply work—I have resisted going with theory at all costs. Of course there are other ideas available, and I encourage you to become a budding detective (and student), and discover those relevant for your own sales career. I also encourage you to refer back to this Appendix on a periodic basis (consider making a note in your calendar to come back to it every 3 months and see if anything has changed for the better). Also know that repetition (through re-reading and practice) is a great way to pick-up on things you might have missed first time around. Enjoy!

The Connecting Habit (Aligning With People)

1. The Connection Key
2. Building Teamwork

The Eliminating Habit (Crushing Unwanted Traits)

3. Removing Fears
4. Extinguishing Excuses
5. Busting Procrastination

The Creating Habit (Developing Lasting Traits)

6. Mastering Time

Chapter 1:
The Connection Key

1. Definition: *connection* is the basic human need we all have, to feel part of something bigger, something more important and encompassing; it also involves connecting with people at a deeper level that has meaning for all parties.
2. Exercise: you are the only person in the world!
3. Dual Mind: the *actor* (responsible for delivery of the communication/message) and the *observer* (responsible for providing feedback to the actor).
4. Three Brains: the *reptilian brain* is the oldest part of the brain and is responsible for what many people understand as the "flight or fight" response. The *mammalian brain* is responsible for relationships and the emotional and intellectual subconscious, and is commonly known as the "feeling brain." Lastly, the *primate brain* is responsible for language, abstract

thought, consciousness, and imagination, and is known as the "logical brain."

5. Assumptionator: is the tool used to recognize, unearth and eventually quash all assumptions.
6. Storyteller: is our innate ability to tell and remember stories, both in our business and personal lives.
7. Silencer: is a mental trigger that alerts the speaker to stay quiet and actively listen to the other person.

Summary

1. Customers prefer to buy from people they have a connection with. It's not impossible to sell without a connection, but you are immediately disadvantaged in comparison to those who choose connection first.
2. Making a connection happens differently for different people—learn the five essential tools for connection until you can instinctively and automatically use the right tool at the right time.
3. Connection is extremely important to kick-start a relationship, but is equally important to maintain throughout the entire relationship. Invest the time to connect during every interaction.

Remember Only This

"Choose to CONNECT first!"

Chapter 2:
Building Teamwork

1. Definition: *teamwork* is where a group of people are brought together willingly, around a common challenge shared by all, to create a solution beneficial to all.
2. Quote: "Nothing worthwhile was every accomplished by someone alone!"
3. Benefits of teamwork:
    1. Eliminates competition earlier.
    2. Shows a strong up-front customer commitment.
    3. Brings in a fun, competitive team spirit.
    4. Aids internal communication and coordination.
    5. Builds your reputation as a team player.
    6. Generates better, and more, ideas.
    7. Delivers faster throughput of actions.
    8. Delegates actions to the best people for the job.
    9. Shows the customer the depth of your internal support team.
    10. Hones your management and teamwork skills.
4. Options to teamwork:
    1. Go it alone.
    2. Delegate responsibility.
    3. Let the customer direct you.
    4. Create an internal team.
    5. Create an external team.
    6. Create a customer-centered team.
    7. Procrastinate (don't).
5. Creating a new team:
    1. Choose great team members.
    2. Explain the value proposition(s) through their eyes.
    3. Bring the team together regularly.
    4. Encourage equal and active participation.
    5. Continually motivate the team.
    6. Disband the team on successful completion.

Summary

1. Teamwork is an action-centered approach, which should be considered frequently to allow faster completion and higher-quality output.
2. Teamwork takes extra effort compared to other options, but when used wisely, yields an output far greater than any individual could ever achieve.
3. Consider recruiting the customer to your team as often as practical, since in so doing you create a stronger connection, gain greater insight, and potentially generate a competitive and winning advantage.

Remember Only This

"Teamwork is about going it TOGETHER!"

Chapter 3:
Removing Fears

1. Definition: *fear* is your amazing imagination working at full power, to transport you magically into the future, and somehow gain predictive powers that let you know what will happen to you.
2. Questions to ask when fear arises:
   1. Why does my mind fire up so quickly and have an immediate need to try and predict the future?
   2. Are my fears unique only to me?
   3. Why do I have predominantly negative thoughts and not positive ones?
   4. Why does this reaction cause even more debilitating negative thoughts?
   5. Why do I not take positive, affirmative action immediately to stem the mind-storm?

6. Why have I done this all my life without having solved it, since it happens so frequently?
7. Is it possible to remove my fears permanently?
8. Am I really going crazy?

3. The Fear-Accepting Program: the mind trigger that catches the fear-thought immediately and allows you to become curious about it, and thus not allowing it to take root in your mind.

4. The Fear-Removing Program: the mind trigger that catches the fear-thought immediately and says "NO" to it, and instead changes the thought to be a positive one from your visions and goals.

5. The most common sales fears:
   1. I will get fired.
   2. People will think I am not good enough.
   3. I will not hit my budget this year.
   4. I will not earn as much as I want or need.
   5. I will need to find a new job.
   6. I won't be able to win this customer.
   7. The competition is too tough.
   8. I will not get promoted.
   9. I am not as good as I think I am.
   10. The business environment is getting tougher every day.
   11. I will go bankrupt.
   12. My peer group is too smart and experienced.
   13. I won't be able to get the price I need.
   14. People will never call me back.
   15. I won't hit all my objectives this year.
   16. I won't be able to recover in time.
   17. I am going to lose this business now.
   18. I won't be able to find new customers.
   19. I won't be able to book that meeting.
   20. People won't like me.

Summary

1. Fears are normal human emotions; start by recognizing and accepting them in real time, then slowly building up to eradicating them.
2. Fears are the biggest catalyst of inaction in a professional salesperson; removing them frees up huge amounts of positive energy that can be applied to growing your business.
3. Removing fears and benefiting from this output is the biggest determinant of sales success bar none.

Remember Only This

"Conquer your fears—it's in you to do so now!"

Chapter 4:
Extinguishing Excuses

1. Definition: an *excuse* is simply where you seek to justify or defend a position or opinion you have, which ultimately STOPS you from taking action—it's an action stopper!
2. A simple process when someone makes an excuse:
   1. Inform.
   2. Encourage.
   3. Ask.
   4. Alert.
   5. Resist.
3. My top ten sales excuses:
   1. I got caught in traffic.
   2. My phone is having problems.
   3. My e-mail crashed—again.
   4. I was sick.
   5. I missed the plane.

6. I am too busy.
7. I'll do it later.
8. Let me think about it.
9. I'll get back to you.
10. It's not my responsibility.

4. Options to excuse making:
    1. Think before you talk.
    2. Ask clarification questions.
    3. One problem, one solution.
    4. "Man on the moon" check.
    5. Outcome visioning.
    6. Challenge assumptions.

Summary

1. Becoming aware of excuses and excuse making, both in you and in others, is the first concrete step toward eliminating them.

2. Be aware that every excuse comes with underlying reasons, or catalysts, for the excuse making in the first place. Professional salespeople know the significant benefits to be realized by unearthing these reasons and using them ethically to their benefit.

3. Excuse making, although deep-rooted, can be stopped and a newer, better approach of taking positive action developed with a little patience and effort on your part!

Remember Only This

"Stop making excuses!"

Author's note: If you are interested I would like to invite you to submit one to three of your best sales-related excuses at http://

www.SalesLeadership.com/BestSalesExcuses. Once I sort and collate them, I will then send you an electronic copy of the completed *Book of Sales Excuses*. You can choose to have your name added as the "author of the excuse" (for fun) or to keep the input anonymous. It should make for some interesting and fun reading!

Chapter 5:
Busting Procrastination

1. Definition: *procrastination* is the action of delaying or postponing something.
2. The four outcomes of procrastination:
   1. You procrastinate once, and then when the thought or requirement to review the action happens again, you choose to start the action.
   2. You procrastinate once, then again, then potentially multiple times, until the action becomes so critical, that not completing it now would cause trouble for you or others. You then start the action.
   3. You procrastinate once, then again, then potentially multiple times, until the action is no longer critical and decide it no longer needs to be completed (phew!)
   4. You procrastinate once, twice, thrice, and in fact continue to procrastinate ad infinitum. The action never gets done, and the procrastination, excuse making, etc., continues indefinitely.
3. Exercise: the big rocks!
4. Typical sales procrastinations:
   1. I am not really sure how to tackle this action.
   2. I've never done this before.
   3. I am not sure how long this action will take.
   4. I know the outcome will not be positive when this is done.
   5. I won't be able to find all the resources I need.
   6. It's probably more hassle than it's worth.
   7. This will only lead to more actions.
   8. I have other higher priority actions.

9. If I leave it, it might go away.
10. I need more information before I start.

5. Procrastination busting mastery tips:
   1. Act on the big rocks early in your day.
   2. Action the smaller, less energy intensive, actions later in your day.
   3. Bring daily awareness to your procrastinations, by noting them down in your Day-Timer system.

Summary

1. Procrastination is a normal, inherent condition in all humans but gets significantly stronger when it is allowed to develop unchecked.
2. Resolving procrastination requires both a system and a daily check-in, and the continuous use of patience to stop the triggers that start it in the first place.
3. You will immediately receive significant benefits, and in many forms, by tackling procrastination immediately.

Remember Only This
"Just do it now!"

Chapter 6:
Mastering Time

1. Definition: *time* is the indefinite continued progress of existence and events in the past, present, and future, regarded as a whole.
2. Measuring your work time usage:
   1. E-mail management.
   2. Travel time.
   3. Sales/management/internal meetings.
   4. Networking/prospecting.

5. Customer visits.
6. Proposal generation.
7. Customer research.
8. Thinking/creative time.
9. Break time (including breakfast, lunches, coffee's, etc.).
10. Miscellaneous (all the other time absorbing things that seem to happen in a typical day).

3. Time buckets (high level):
   1. Working time.
   2. Commuting time.
   3. Family time.
   4. Hobby time.
   5. "Me" time.
   6. Sleep time.
   7. Etc.

4. Time bucket key questions:
   1. Do I have the right number of time bucket categories to begin with?
   2. Do I have a priority attached to each time bucket, knowing what ones are the most important?
   3. Do I have the right number of hours in each of the time buckets to achieve life balance?
   4. Do I have enough hours in my work time bucket to allow me to achieve all my sales goals?
   5. Am I willing to have flexibility by using time from another bucket if I am short of hours in my working time bucket?
   6. If I "borrow" time from one bucket in a given week to use in another, do I replace that time in future weeks?

5. How *The 80/20 Rule* can manifest itself in your sales career:
   1. Eighty percent of revenues will come from twenty percent of your total work time.
   2. Eighty percent of revenues will come from twenty percent of your total number of customers.

6. Excuses for not implementing *The 80/20 Rule*:
   1. You need the low-revenue customers to have the high-revenue customers.

2. The high-revenue customers come from working all the customers, and seeing which ones filter to the top.
3. Nobody can have an unfair proportion of high-revenue customers.
4. You need to keep working the low-revenue customers in case some of the high-revenue ones disappear.
5. Business is tough, so I cannot drop any of my low-revenue customers.

7. Time mastery best practices:
   1. Know your goals in as much detail as possible.
   2. Find quiet time and a creative thinking place.
   3. Understand that actions are always time.
   4. Realize what is random and what is not.
   5. Build in "slack" time.
   6. Learn the discipline of time blocking.
   7. Be ruthless with e-mail.
   8. Develop the skill of knowing how long actions take to complete.
   9. Learn to say NO!
   10. Start your day off consistently (the best possible way).

Summary

1. Learn the skills, and develop the disciplines, of measuring and categorizing your time, and how to balance your various time buckets.
2. Use *The 80/20 Rule* to concentrate on smart time, which always turns out to be the most impactful, positive, and results-generating time.
3. Become an unceasing student of time mastery, and incorporate the tips and tricks of the time masters, the highest performers of the sales world.

Remember Only This

"Mastering time is the foundation of all success!"

Chapter 7:
Creating Momentum

1. Definition: *momentum* is the outcome of applied force that creates positive movement.
2. The building blocks of momentum:
   1. There has to be a clear goal, or set of goals, at the outset that will harness the motivation to take action.
   2. Action needs to happen once the goal is clear—without focused action, movement toward your goal will be erratic at best.
   3. It would appear easy to stop action once started, since impatience or other factors could easily creep in, and suggest the needed results are not materializing quickly enough. Resist the urge to quit or change approach, and instead stay focused and keep doing the *right things at the right time*.
   4. Results start materializing and your goals start being achieved. At this stage it would be wise to uncover what actions are required to keep momentum going at the pace you desire.
   5. As you reach the pinnacle of hitting your goals consistently, be humble and thankful for your achievements. This will help you keep your eye on the subsequent actions required, and stop possible complacency.
3. A simple approach to creating momentum:
   1. Develop a clear understanding of the goal(s) and outcome(s) you are seeking.
   2. Determine opportunities for leverage.
   3. Implement the actions one by one.
   4. Practice patience.
   5. Check in against your goals and outcomes to date.

6. Challenge yourself on acceleration ideas at this stage.
7. Be comfortable during the flow of momentum.
4. Definition of the momentum master key: *leverage* is the power to influence a person or situation to achieve a desired outcome or goal.
5. Types of leverage:
   1. Ethical leverage.
   2. Unethical leverage.
6. Putting the brakes on momentum:
   1. Not having a clear, consistent vision or strategy that stands the test of time.
   2. Not having the courage to start something because of an excuse, or excuses, that you think cannot be overcome.
   3. Not having the patience to stick with both strategy and actions to break through the barriers to success.
   4. Becoming arrogant and taking your eye off the ball as you begin to see some early signs of success.
   5. Abandoning what has worked successfully for you in the past by chasing something that you think is a lot easier (the principle of getting something for nothing!).
7. Ten ideas to help create momentum:
   1. Time block—it helps with consistency in applying actions.
   2. Recount and promote successes—they are fuel for the *Law of Attraction*.
   3. Laugh at apparent failures—spend less time thinking about them and more on positive action.
   4. Seek out people who are momentum and success conscious—they are contagious.
   5. Choose to do something every day toward your goals, no matter how small the action.
   6. For every strategy and action think about the potential of leverage in some way.
   7. Don't deviate from your strategy.
   8. Keep your eyes open for synchronicities (these are coincidences you decide to take action on).

9. Create light process as you go along—make them simple, highly repeatable and easy to implement.
10. Simply believe that you can do it—employ daily positive affirmations—they do work if you try them!

Summary

1. Everyone creates momentum to some degree or other; raise your own bar and use the concept of momentum to achieve more goals, with more sustainable results, and faster than ever before.
2. Understanding the concept of leverage and applying it to every opportunity, provides for massive acceleration towards the achievement of your goals through increased momentum.
3. Know that creating and maintaining momentum is a process that can and should be learned early, and applied as often as possible.

Remember Only This
"Leverage creates momentum to achieve
your goals faster!"

Chapter 8:
Manifesting Synchronicities

1. Definition: a *synchronicity* is a coincidence that you pro-actively think about and decide to take positive and affirmative action on.
2. How many synchronicities can I manifest? It's infinite and is a direct function of how positive you consistently think and act.
3. What stops synchronicities from happening:
   1. Thinking negatively.
   2. Counting synchronicities.

3. Choosing not to share benefits.
4. Choosing not to act on coincidences.
5. Trying to force synchronicities to materialize.
6. Thinking of scarcity.
7. Not following your personal vision and goals.
4. Steps to manifest synchronicity:
    1. Think positively.
    2. Believe in the abundance model.
    3. Stay positive.
    4. Be continually thankful.
    5. Don't get cocky or arrogant.
    6. They appear cyclical—don't get discouraged.
    7. Follow your life's true purpose.
    8. Take action!

Summary

1. Coincidences happen to everyone. Choosing to positively act on them can create synchronicities and through this highly beneficial outcomes.
2. Synchronicities appear to happen in waves. Have your surfboard ready and waiting!
3. Manifesting further synchronicities in your life requires trust in the universe and an undying positive attitude under all circumstances.

Remember Only This

"Think and act on a coincidence, then watch the synchronicity manifest itself!"

Chapter 9:
Selling Values

1. Definition: *personal values* are the set of guides that are intrinsic to me as a human being, that stay with me at all times, and always let me know "the right thing to do."
2. Ten recommendations for thinking about values:
   1. Never, ever compromise on integrity.
   2. Exhibit transparency in all your business interactions.
   3. Chose to care about your customers and their success.
   4. Communicate in a timely manner.
   5. Treat all people with dignity and respect.
   6. Listen, listen, and listen again.
   7. Choose to see the best in people.
   8. Believe in the concept of abundance, not scarcity.
   9. Develop and practice perseverance and tenacity.
   10. Do what you *intrinsically* know is right.

Summary

1. Think about, and be crystal clear on what your own values are; when people ask you about them, don't be wishy-washy!
2. Discovering and aligning with a customer's values can create a lasting connection with them.
3. Alignment of values with your customers can create significant competitive advantage for you.

Remember Only This

"Embrace values, be consistent with them, and take the time to discover them in other people!"

Chapter 10:
Binding Propositions

1. Definition: *binding propositions* require that to sell anything—whether a product, service, or even yourself—requires the other person (the buyer) to be interested enough in what is being offered, that they agree to buy from you.
2. Types of value propositions:
   1. A personal value proposition that allows him to create and maintain amazing connection with the prospective buyer.
   2. A company value proposition that highlights both credibility and worthiness of his company, allowing them to appear highly suitable.
   3. One or more product or service value propositions that solve real-world problems for customers, and are so compelling that they are chosen over competitive solutions.
   4. Four key steps to building a product or service value proposition:
      1. Collection phase.
      2. Benefits phase.
      3. Differentiated benefits phase.
      4. End-user differentiated benefits phase.

Summary

1. Data and information are transformed into benefits, and benefits transformed into value propositions when they confer an advantage, convenience or service to your customer. It's that simple!
2. Product and service value propositions are developed through a clear four-step process. Develop the skills necessary for every step, and remember not to make the most common mistake of stopping after completion of Step 3!

3. Value proposition creation is a mind-set that must be mastered by the professional salesperson. It includes personal, company, product and service value propositions, which must all be congruent to each other.

Remember Only This

"See the world through the eyes of your customer!"

Chapter 11:
Powerfully Influencing

1. Definition: *influencing* can be considered as the process of moving a person's opinion from one state to another, with this new state being the required one that brings them to the point of "being convinced," and of course being convinced in your favor!
2. Four reasons why influencing may be required:
   1. A lack of knowledge or understanding of your value proposition, that requires further information.
   2. The challenge of obtaining enough information from you, which can then be compared against other competing solutions.
   3. A current position that is in favor of a competitive solution.
   4. A clear understanding of your current value proposition, that puts the customer in a strong position to ask even more from you.
3. The different types of negative influencing:
   1. Fear (of something important to the prospective customer).
   2. Threatening (of something of value to the prospective customer).
   3. Withholding (of something necessary for the prospective customer).
   4. Extorting (of something of value to the nonprofessional salesperson).

4. Ten options to ethically influence:
   1. Seek to uncover, and deal only in facts.
   2. Build from common ground, strengthening the foundation.
   3. Embrace differences of opinion openly.
   4. Allow proper time for the influencing process to progress.
   5. Encourage open and constructive debate.
   6. Don't expect to have all the answers immediately.
   7. Keep track of what has been agreed to, ideally in writing.
   8. Be truthful, even with unavoidable bad news.
   9. Encourage a long-term partnership approach.
   10. Be timely in the completion of all actions and communication.

Summary

1. Influencing is a necessary and expected part of most sales transactions, expected both by the professional salesperson and the prospective customer alike.
2. Influencing is both a skill and an art, which can be mastered through study, practice and repetition.
3. When influencing another, influence in a way that you would consider fair and ethical if the roles were reversed.

Remember Only This

"Always influence ethically!"

Chapter 12:
Igniting Initiative

1. Definition of initiative (some options):
   1. The ability to assess and initiate things independently.
   2. The power, or ability, to act or take charge before others do.

3. An act, or strategy, designed to resolve a difficulty, or improve a situation; a fresh approach.
2. Initiative and energy are intimately intertwined!
3. Things that can stop initiative in its tracks:
    1. Fear.
    2. Laziness.
    3. Procrastination.
    4. Excuse making.
    5. Illness.
    6. Tiredness.
4. Things that can cause initiative to be out of your control:
    1. Rules and regulations.
    2. Implied expectations.
    3. Industry or social norms.
4. You work in a micromanaged environment.
5. Key sales skills to ignite initiative:
    1. Dream really, really big.
    2. Surround yourself with like-minded individuals.
    3. Get into a positive routine.
    4. Employ a coach or mentor.
    5. Work for yourself or a truly great company.
    6. Develop challenging hobbies outside of work.
    7. Be a student of sales teachings.
    8. Put yourself out there!

Summary

1. Understanding and taking initiative is the lifeblood of being in sales, and truly igniting initiative will, over time, become a key differentiator in your career.
2. Choosing to ignite initiative brings with it so many other significant benefits, including increased positivity, heightened creativeness, and also higher energy reserves to simply get more done.

3. Learn to have complete control over your personal initiative, and realize that there are times to really apply it, and times to keep it in reserve until you are time-balanced once more.

Remember Only This

"Initiative is your rocket fuel for action taking!"

Chapter 13:
Balance Mastery: The Sales Habit Way

1. Definition: *balance* is what you think and want it to be!
2. The four major types of balance:
   a. Physical.
   b. Mental.
   c. Emotional.
   d. Spiritual.
3. The six key characteristics of sales balance:
   a. Courage.
   b. Motivation.
   c. Energy-conscious.
   d. Strategic thinking.
   e. Discipline.
   f. A sense of humor.
4. The six key skills of sales balance:
   a. Planning.
   b. Bouncing back.
   c. Recharging.
   d. Outside interests.
   e. Relaxing/quiet times.
   f. Giving back.

Summary

1. Balance is worthy of the effort it takes to achieve it.
2. Balance is without doubt a competitive advantage you have against all those salespeople who choose not to have it in their lives.
3. Balance will allow you to become a more complete person, enjoying success in all aspects of your life and not just in your sales career.

Remember Only This

"Balance, and through this happiness, is the ultimate goal of sales habit mastery"

CLOSING COMMENTS

You made it—congratulations! I hope you were entertained, intrigued, encouraged to think and reflect, and ultimately took away a nugget or two of practical information that once implemented in your sales role will yield something quite special for you.

I encourage you to become a lifelong student of sales and the many interesting subjects associated with it. There is much to learn from great teachers and successful practitioners alike that can rapidly accelerate your sales career and success. I also encourage you to become a sales detective, from the standpoint of further developing your inquiring mind. The best sales professionals I have ever worked with have always had a healthy, inquiring mind and always seemed to ask that additional question, the one that somehow illuminated a situation and brought additional success.

Lastly, I encourage you to seek out a professional mentor or sales coach who can work closely with you, as someone on your team, giving you a distinct advantage over your peers. They will guide you at a pace acceptable to you, be rooting for your continued success, and helping you achieve it even faster. It's worth the small investment and will undoubtedly magnify your positive results when you find the right one.

You can contact me, and also find additional details of *The 6 Sales Habits* workbook, online training course, blogs, and related information at: **http://www.The6SalesHabits.com**

My best wishes to you!
Joe Connelly
CEO and Founder, SalesLeadership.com

ABOUT THE AUTHOR

With a highly successful, and varied, international sales career, spanning over 28 years, Joe has learned the real-world lessons that make both a great sales professional and a great sales executive.

Having worked in small, mid, and large-size companies, including both product and service companies, he shares his wisdom of sales in a way that is easy to understand, steeped in real-world practicality, and ultimately reveals what is really important in today's ever-changing business environment.

He strongly believes that achieving long-term, sustainable success in sales is something that can be learned and can be implemented quickly by those willing to seek higher performance.

Joe lives in Switzerland, enjoying the amazing hiking, chocolate, and coffee and is happy being a professional writer, speaker, executive coach, and troubleshooting consultant for all things sales related. He can be reached directly at **connectwithjoe@ SalesLeadership.com**

You can contact me, and also find additional details of *The 12 Guides of Sales Leadership* workbook, online training course, blogs, and related information at: **http://www.The12GuidesOfSalesLeadership.com**

You can contact me, and also find additional details of *The Holistic Executive* workbook, online training course, blogs, and related information at: **http://www.TheHolisticExecutive.com**